JOURNAL FOR THE STUDY OF THE OLD TESTAMENT
SUPPLEMENT SERIES
14

Editors
David J A Clines
Philip R Davies
David M Gunn

Department of Biblical Studies
The University of Sheffield
Sheffield S10 2TN
England

THE FATE OF KING SAUL

An Interpretation of a Biblical Story

DAVID M. GUNN

Journal for the Study of the Old Testament
Supplement Series, 14

Sheffield 1980

ISSN 0309-0787
ISBN 0 905774 24 8

Published by
JSOT Press
Department of Biblical Studies
The University of Sheffield
Sheffield S10 2TN
England

Printed in Great Britain
by Redwood Burn Limited
Trowbridge & Esher
1980

To Margaret, my wife

CONTENTS

PREFACE

My hope is that this book might prove of interest not only to those who make the study of the Old Testament their profession but also to others who come to the story of Saul from a variety of backgrounds. I have in mind, for example, the student of literature (probably English Literature) who will no doubt have been told often enough that the Bible is a "literary masterpiece" but who, when seeking to explore further, may have been surprised to find a certain paucity of critical assistance from the "professionals". To the reader who has been gripped by Sophocles' King Oedipus, Shakespeare's Macbeth, or Hardy's Tess of the d'Urbervilles, I suggest that the story of Saul might profitably be next on the reading programme, and I offer here some lines of thought and feeling which are my own response to this fine example of Hebrew narrative art. Or perhaps the pastor who has preached, if not specifically on Saul's sin and rejection, at least on the providence of God, might find something here to give pause and prompt some serious reflection. The story of King Saul is, I believe, one of the Bible's "uncomfortable" stories.

In the interests of general readability I have tried to keep the technicalities of scholarship to a minimum. At least that was my intention at the outset. Looking now at the finished product I wonder whether I have succeeded. And since I envisage any "non-professional" audience to be English speaking, I have mainly drawn attention to English-language books and articles, where they are relevant to the discussion. My apologies to readers in other language traditions. Reference to secondary literature is by author's name and, if necessary, date of publication. A complete list of such works is found in the Bibliography at the end of the book. Quotations from the Bible generally follow the RSV translation, though sometimes with my own modifications.

9

My thanks, as always with a project like this, are due to many people. In particular I am grateful to my colleagues here in Sheffield, David Clines, Philip Davies and John Rogerson, who all offered helpful criticisms and induced me to make some significant modifications. Especially valuable, too, have been the many stimulating discussions I have had on the subject with my student, Lorraine King; indeed, it has become a little difficult sometimes to sort out the extent of my indebtedness to her (though I don't blame her for the result!). But in particular I am grateful to her for drawing my attention to some of the symbolism in the story (for example, concerning clothes), for suggestions on the actions and character of Samuel, and for pressing me to think further about the significance of Saul's "confession" of sin and God's "repentance" (1 Samuel 15). She also convinces me (too late to modify my text) that my assessment of the character of Jonathan should allow for a somewhat larger element of "calculation" and less simple "naïveté". Perhaps she will publish her own assessment one day.

Finally I owe the book to two people whose contribution is quite other. To Gordon Owen whose love of literature I still feed on; and to my wife, Margaret, who in her own way sustained its writing, who is for me the gift of Providence, and to whom I dedicate the book.

David Gunn
Department of Biblical Studies
The University of Sheffield

March, 1980

Introduction
BIBLICAL STORY AND LITERARY CRITIC

It is my belief that much Old Testament narrative belongs naturally to the life-sphere of art and entertainment and that to approach this material as a literary critic might an epic poem, a novel or a play, can be helpful to the modern reader. Well to say that is hardly to break new ground.[1] So let me say a little more in the hope of being useful, at least in giving some indication of how I wish to approach the subject of this book.

So many Old Testament stories seem to me to embody a desire to capture and hold an audience, through the creation of tension and relief, the provoking of laughter and tears, the moulding of thoughts and words into soothing, startling, pleasing or simply decorous shapes. Ask the "man in the street" what he knows of the Old Testament and chances are that high on the list (which will probably be a short one!) will come some of the best narratives - of Jacob and Joseph, Moses and David. If many Old Testament stories began life as entertainment so too have they sustained life as entertainment.

But, as we all know, there is entertainment and entertainment. So I borrow the term "serious" from Matthew Arnold who once spoke of the artistry of the finest poets in terms of its "high seriousness". "Serious" entertainment (be it comic or tragic or whatever) grips one and challenges one to self- or social-reassessment. It has (to risk another phrase) a moral dimension. This I believe to be true of the Old Testament. My concern in this present book, then, is with a particular narrative, the story of King Saul, as literary entertainment of high seriousness, of moral probity. An

11

appropriate mode of analysis might therefore involve more than "aesthetics" but be concerned with discrimination and evaluation at both aesthetic and moral levels.

Obviously one of the dimensions of seriousness in Old Testament narrative is likely to be a theological dimension. It is not the only such dimension but it is an important one and clearly it is of major concern to many readers and most commentators. Nevertheless, it is helpful in discussing such literature to bear in mind that if the "theological" aspect indicates the "seriousness" of the literature, the story also embodies principles of aesthetics and enjoyment. In Old Testament studies critics have (in my view) sometimes too readily viewed these stories as simply prescriptive of a particular kind of seriousness - theological, political, historical - and, just because they are fundamentally only interested in prescriptions, read a drastically simplistic "message" or "purpose" from the narrative. Some serious entertainment does offer simple categories of "comment" and succeeds in doing so; more often it deals in complexity and ambiguity. Literature that reads like a theological tract or a political pamphlet has generally a short life as entertainment. The critic whose primary interest is in the theological or political-historical dimensions of an Old Testament story might usefully take due cognizance of the aesthetic/entertainment dimension of a narrative and consider whether in reading off prescriptions he or she is not unduly ironing out the enlivening ambiguities or "openness" of the text.

But before I can start my own exploration of the Saul story there are one or two preliminary questions to be dealt with briefly.

For a start, what is my text? It is a section of narrative from within the books of Samuel. But is it a proper "unit"? Yes, depending on how one defines the term "unit". Old Testament scholars have become accustomed to see "units" in terms of the "sources", "traditions" or "literary forms" which were drawn upon by authors/editors in the making of a biblical book. It is not the only way of usefully defining a literary unit in a biblical book. That depends on what the critic is setting out to do. I have written elsewhere (1978) on what I like to call the "Story of King David", arguing that what I am interpreting is substantially a self-contained "original" unit of material which has been incorporated, more or less as it stands, into its present context in the books of Samuel and Kings. Well and good, as long as the reader is prepared to accept my definition of what constitutes the original boundaries of the story, a matter which is far from being beyond dispute. On the other hand, in what I wish to say here about the story of King Saul - partly because I do not believe that anyone has succeeded in delineating the constituent sources of 1 Samuel[2] and partly because I happen to be interested this time in the "final form" of the text - I shall take as my focus of attention the narrative about Saul as it stands and not attempt to establish the relationship of this narrative to its putative sources. To be sure, I am imposing my own precise boundaries (beginning and end) on the text. That is to say, I am defining the literary unit without claiming that it necessarily once had a distinct life of its own in precisely that form. But I would argue that these boundaries are not entirely arbitrary; on the contrary, the resultant text could be shown (a) to conform to various conventions of story-telling (with, for example, situation, complication, resolution and aftermath), (b) to display internal coherence, and (c) to be amenable to an empirical test of what might constitute the "story of Saul" (namely, try it on your friends!).[3]

Let me clarify: I am not suggesting that questions of constituent sources, redactional alterations, etc., are in principle of no value. If we wish to know something of the history of a text and perhaps something of the history of the ideas and thought-forms which are incorporated in it, then they are obviously indispensable.[4] When it comes, however, to reading the text in the form in which we have it now, seeking an integrated interpretation, it is not surprising to find such discussion to be often of relatively little assistance.[5] Unless the compilation of the material has been made purely mechanically, or redactional material inserted that is totally out of sympathy with the "basic" material, then it is likely that there will be an overall flow and coherence in the final product - and this is what I have found in looking closely at the Saul story.

The only significant difficulty with the plot lies in the abrupt juxtaposition of the two stories of David's introduction to court (1 Samuel 16 and 17), though in practice this "gap" can be bridged with merely the smallest suspension of disbelief. As for difficulties at the level of "meaning" in the sense of "message" or "values", my assessment is that where redaction critics (that is, critics concerned with the contributions of editors, "redactors") discern the hand of DtrN, DtrP or whoever, the passage in question may usually be seen to underline or strengthen an already existing element in the (postulated) basic story-material - for example, David's restraint and freedom from bloodguilt, Jonathan's acquiescence in David's rise to kingship, a less than fawning attitude to the monarchy, or an interest in the authority of the prophetic word. In a sense, then, these touches of "propaganda" (if that is what they are, originally) are digested and become part of the story as a whole.

That is not to say that there are not tensions within the narrative. On the contrary, it is the presence of genuinely competing perspectives or value-systems that makes literature most challenging, and this, as far as I am concerned, is certainly the case with the Saul story. In speaking of "flow" and "coherence" I am simply claiming that these tensions, some of which may be due to redaction, are subsumed (which does not necessarily mean eliminated) in a complex but artistically satisfying whole. That this is the case with the Saul material is, of course, an assertion inviting critical demonstration - which is what the rest of the book is about.

Perhaps a more difficult theoretical matter for the "final-form" critic concerns the story's matrix. In what I shall say here about the story of Saul I shall largely leave out of consideration its relation to the books of Samuel as a whole as well as to the larger "Deuteronomistic History" (Deuteronomy to 2 Kings) which scholars posit as a single and coherent unit (drawn from many "sources") of which our story is but a small part. In this respect my discussion is, in principle, deficient. Perhaps an overview of the greater unit would push into the background certain elements which I find to be prominent and vice versa. My defence is that variety is the spice of life. Just as different methodological starting points can only enhance our view of the nature and function of the Bible, so in considering a large work, using broadly a single method, it can be valuable to employ different starting points - moving from smaller constituent units (many of which may overlap) to the larger entity and vice versa.

But the difficulty does not end here. By talking of the "Deuteronomistic History" I invite the question, Just whose narrative precisely is it that you are writing about? When you write about the meaning of the text are you specifying some particular author's intention? To these questions I have no easy answers. The problem of authorial intentionality is complicated enough with literature where the author is known. With Old Testament narrative it is vastly more complicated by the facts (a) that most ascriptions of particular authorship, as well as of date and circumstances of composition, are heavily notional and (b) that most narrative (the Saul story is clearly a case in point) is the product of composite authorship. One cannot simply speak of the author being the last redactor since the last redactor may not have been the last substantial redactor (and is a redactor really the same as an author?) - and so the difficulties multiply.

My own response to the question lies in the direction of minimizing talk of particular authorial intentionality and of conceiving authorship in broader terms, thinking of the author as a kind of super-ego, if you like, linked to all who have left their mark on the story. If indeed our text has a rich redactional history (howbeit untraceable in detail), then what I see as its coherence is the product of a process of interaction between, on the one hand, the stuff of the story (not only elements of plot and character but insights and values already resident in it at any given stage of redaction or compilation) and, on the other hand, those who have grappled with it (the author[s], redactors, etc.). Their contributions have shaped the story. The story has shaped their contributions. When I find subtlety in this story it is not necessarily the deliberate contrivance of a master narrator that I am exposing, though that may also be the case; rather it may be a subtlety created unconsciously in the dialectical process by which the story is created, a subtlety which is the logical resolution of the variously nuanced contributions and not a property of the contributions themselves.

Thus I think it important that the story may be thought of as having a certain life of its own - a universality of discourse - which can be probed and appropriated independently of particular author and/or intention. It is some such underlying assumption of universality that has allowed these texts to continue to have a life as serious entertainment up to the present day, and I would suggest that some such assumption needs to go on being made if the texts are to have an existential function in the future.[6]

Inevitably such talk will prompt accusations of "subjectivity", as though subjectivity were not a major matter to be reckoned with in the proliferating hypotheses of sources, tradition-history, authorship and socio-historical context. Perhaps what is at issue here is more fundamental than an argument over precise method. Rather it concerns one's understanding of one's role as critic. Many Old Testament scholars have liked to seek and find for their work a model in the physical sciences. There is also room, I believe, for an unashamed assertion of humanism in our discipline - for a view of the critic as one whose most important task is to discriminate between, and mediate, aesthetic and moral values.[7]

This is heady talk and it is tempting to indulge it further. But while recognizing that it is important for a critic to have thought through some of the main theoretical implications of his or her approach I am not persuaded that every scholar needs to be a philosopher of method. That is a valuable role for some to assume, but there is a danger that when the commonality of critics (in which I include myself) is absorbed by the deep puzzlements of "methodology" all too little actual criticism (interpretation, exegesis, or what you will) of the text gets done.

Perhaps something of my hesitation to theorize derives from my experience (a good many years ago) as a student reading English Literature. As the end of the course approached I grew increasingly restless over precisely this question: what was it that we were really doing as "critics" of literature? It was the one subject no one talked about. How one performed as critic, yes, but not the fundamental "hermeneutical" question. My moment came with an option in the final year: I (and two others) took a course on the History and Theory of Criticism; the other forty or so in the class took some more exotic option (Australian literature, it was, I believe). It was a good course, fascinating, but frustrating. Alas, Aristotle and Longinus, Sidney and Johnson (etc., etc.) all had insights but none seemed to have any truly satisfactory answer that served for now as well as for then. Frustrating, but in time illuminating; for it allowed me to see that in the last analysis it was the critical practice that counted. It is not the theory of criticism that I look back on with gratitude but the critical essays of Empson and Leavis (amongst others) and of Johnson, for that matter.

Bound up with this point about criticism is another which is encapsulated for me in another experience (not such a number of years ago) when I was quizzed on a "literary" essay which I had written on an Old Testament text. My interlocutor was puzzled by the essay, understandably as I see it now, inasmuch as it offered an interpretation but not the usual massive sets of "evidence" or "argument" so familiar in the products of Old Testament studies. How had I gone about the analysis? Where was my "working", my "sifting of evidence"? Had I tried other themes (other than the one I was exploring in the essay)? How had I settled on this one? He seemed only to want to know how I arrived at my interpretation; I wanted to know whether he found it stimulating or not! Again a somewhat teasing experience but a profitable one.

My answer to such questioning is, Yes, you see the outcome of a lot of "trying on for size", using various time-honoured techniques[8] but also relying a good deal on intuition at various points in the process. One isolates certain "prima facie" lines of interpretation and then tests how they fit the text, through and through, modifying, modifying and modifying (and often abandoning!). To set out all such working can be to kill off the essay - to no advantage.[9] For the acid test is whether the interpretation is "workable" - does it illuminate the text? Does it stay with a reader on subsequent readings of the text?

It may be that other critics will proffer (or have proffered already) more convincing interpretations - interpretations which are more consistent, coherent, which throw more light on larger areas of the text, which account more smoothly for more difficulties in the text (and so on) - in which case one's own interpretation will wither away and be discarded. But it may be that it will be found to gel with other interpretations or to go on vying with them - for there is no reason to suppose that there is a single answer to the question, What does this story mean? If an interpretation enjoys some measure of tenacity, however small, in the reader's view, then the critic's endeavour has been worthwhile.

Let me now come more directly to our story.

For purposes of defining the boundaries let me simply assume the beginning of the story with the appearance of Saul (chapter 9) and the end with his death (chapter 31).[10] But the issue of the kingship is so strong in the opening episodes that I see it as essential to include chapter 8 as a prologue, and equally the story of the burial of Saul and the crowning of David as king in Hebron seems to be a fitting epilogue even if the climax of the story has been reached with Saul's death on Gilboa (the anti-climactic aftermath is familiar in traditional stories). The plot then is relatively straightforward. A king is asked for (šā'ûl), promised and chosen in the person of Saul. Saul proves his worth in battle (chapter 11). But there is a complication - in the eyes of the god, Yahweh, and his prophet, Samuel, the king is only king on sufferance. He is still on trial (chapter 12), and indeed he fails the subsequent tests (chapters 13 and 15). His successor, David, is chosen by Yahweh and the remainder of the story depicts Saul's vain struggle for self-preservation by striving to check David's rising fortune. A major sub-plot concerns the king's betrayal by his own family, culminating in Jonathan's abdication as heir to the throne. Finally Saul's death resolves the plot by opening the way for David, without having used violence against Saul, to succeed to the throne.

Commentators on the material which comprises our story of Saul are not slow to recognize in it serious theological interests. While differing purposes are postulated of different sources (for example, pro- or anti-monarchic), usually an account of the story is spelt out along the following lines. The story of Saul is really subordinate to that of David's rise. The interest lies in justifying David as the legitimate king of Israel, that is, sanctioned by Yahweh. Saul is essentially a foil to David.

Biblical Story and Literary Critic

Chosen by Yahweh and endowed with his spirit, Saul nevertheless fails to measure up to the strict standards of obedience to God (through his prophet) demanded of one who is to be king over the people of God. The spirit departs from him and is given to David who is depicted as the model of the true king.

There are other dimensions to this story, however, which are perhaps less often explored. D. H. Lawrence, in his play David, has Saul say, "I am a man given over to trouble and tossed between two winds". Adam Welch, some years ago, wrote of Saul as "a man wrestling with fate and with the dark powers which hem in every man's destiny, which limit him at every point in his effort to reach the thing he has set before him". Both writers (and others have made similar points) see Saul as subject to forces beyond his control. On this reading, then, Saul's failure as king is not simply a matter of obedience or disobedience; nor is the story presented in simple categories of right and wrong, good and evil. Yahweh, in Welch's phrase, is a "dark power".

The following essay is the product of explorations prompted by a growing awareness of these other dimensions.

Part One
SETTING THE SCENE

Since I love him it must be my fate, it must be
my destiny.

Masha

But I've made up my mind. If I can't go to
Moscow, well, I can't, and that's that. It's just
the way things have turned out. It can't be
helped, it's all God's will and that's the truth.

Irina

If we could only know! If we could only know!

Olga

Chekhov, <u>The Three Sisters</u>

Chapter One
SIN AND TRAGEDY

Saul's reputation has been hardly an enviable one, at least in Christian circles. While Jewish tradition has treated this first king of Israel with some sympathy, Christian tradition has shown him a large measure of hostility. Perhaps one of the roots of such hostility lies in the fact that for many early commentators David is seen as both the progenitor of Christ "in the flesh" and the "type" of Christ in terms of his spiritual significance. In a sense, therefore, Saul who persecuted David, persecuted also Christ. Augustine (fourth/fifth century), for example, in his commentary on Psalm 56 sees Saul in his hostility to David as representing the Jews who sought the death of Jesus. For Nicholas of Lyra (twelfth/thirteenth century) Saul is, moreover, the figure of Satan ("not merely as an empty figure of Satan but his instrument at a certain moment on earth"), a type of the persecutor of the Church - in particular of the Roman emperors, Diocletian and Maximianus - and represented, on a moral plane, the "world" (from which David sought to escape) as opposed to the "undiluted goodness of God". Among the Reformers of the sixteenth century Saul is pictured, in contrast to David, as "tied to the law" and, in political theology is persistently exampled as the type of the tyrant/king/magistrate who persecutes true religion and faithful pastors. Thus for Beza, Saul represented the impure and corrupt Valois monarchy and readily provided a parallel to contemporary persecution of religious minorities (through, for example, the story of the massacre of the priests at Nob; cf. Psalm 52).[1] Coming closer to our own time (say the last two hundred years), we can see the same negative evaluation in (Christian) commentator after commentator, particularly in writings with a homiletical or devotional purpose. The story of Saul is to be read as a salutory warning, a lesson about sin and failure. Let us not be like Saul, is the concluding prayer.

In one tradition Saul is utterly to be abhorred (Robinson, 34, 64):[2]

> Awful as the case is, there are not a few, who, to our apprehensions, begin in the Spirit, and end in the flesh. Such was Saul. Let his example be improved as a solemn warning to all, to beware of dissimulation....We wonder not at any the most execrable wickedness, which one, given up to final impenitence, may perpetrate. "Lord, what is man?" What enormities is he capable of committing? From the examples of some obdurate sinners, we perceive, what we ourselves might have been or may still be, if the grace of God prevent not. Let us learn, then, under a sense of our entire depravity, to pray, "Hold thou me up, and I shall be safe: and I will have respect unto thy statutes continually".

The best that can be said of him is that he directs our view to one who is greatly to be emulated (Ridout, 3):

> The subject in one sense is a depressing one, and the proper effect should be to turn us from the contemplation of the man after the flesh [Saul] to the man after God's own heart, David, who...shows the contrast between faith and nature. As a type of Christ, he is the antidote to the baleful example and influence of poor Saul.

Another tradition of exposition condemns yet finds more room for sympathy. While the lesson of Saul's failure retains a central position, it does not wholly displace all hint of identification between the expositor and the failed king (Hastings, 73):

> It is hard to blame Saul for failing in the test which the prophet imposed on him [1 Sam 13], when he persistently delayed till the end of seven days. A severer trial would not have been devised for a man

Sin and Tragedy

with military instincts, who had to watch the opportunity slipping away before his eyes. And Saul nearly stood the test....There was some excuse, considerable temptation, no slight admixture of better motives, some superstition, some sense of the necessity of God's help, much neglect of God's directions as to the proper way of securing it. Saul showed that he could not wait for God in absolute faith that He would not fail or deceive. He was careful to maintain an outward rite, but the spirit of devotion and faith was altogether wanting....He owns to having forced his conscience; he acted against the inward warning; he resisted the Spirit of God; he preferred his own thoughts to the express command of the prophet; he had light and he chose darkness, because his heart was not with God.

Echoes of such exposition are not difficult to find among modern "critical" commentators, even where the style of exposition is less directly homiletic. Hertzberg's account of the "final compilation" of Saul materials (by a "deutero-nomistic compiler") concludes (p. 133):

[Saul] is the anointed; he is loved by many, even by his opponent Samuel, he is pious in the extreme, brave yet modest, without doubt a man of the stuff of which kings are made. But despite his zeal for Yahweh, he appears, in fact, more as the king which other nations have than as the instrument of Yahweh, which the king over the people of God must be. This is the view of ch. 15, and it is the view which the final compiler appropriated and made his own. Here he saw the outcome correctly. Saul is the inauguration of the kingdom. But the king set over the people of God must be a man of God's grace, called by him and a real instrument in his hand. This Saul is not. To this extent, the history of the beginning of the kingdom at the same time also ponders the theological evaluation of the kingdom in Israel. Only the man "on whom the spirit of the Lord shall rest" (Isa. 11.2) can really be the king of Israel. The first king is like a sign pointing toward the true kingly office, but at the same time also a sign showing that

25

the man who holds this office can come to grief in it. Only he who allows God to be wholly king, and who is therefore himself completely obedient, can be king over the people of God. The first king is measured strictly by this standard and cannot come up to it. But he remains the anointed one nevertheless, and continues to bear the insignia of the kingship which have been handed to him; even as rejected king he remains king, the first of the line at the end of which stands the One who alone was completely obedient.

Though the commentator has retained a certain "historical" perspective here - the evaluation of Saul is couched in terms of the final ("deuteronomistic") compiler's assessment of what is demanded by kingship - there is never any significant distance between Hertzberg's description of the compiler's evaluation and his assent to it together with his urging of it upon his reader as a standard which applies to people in general and not just to Israelite kings. This is evident not only from the value judgement at the beginning of the passage ("Here he saw the outcome correctly"), but also from the final sentence which suggests that the story has its ultimate meaning only within the framework of a Christian doctrine of the nature and significance of Jesus the messiah ("anointed king"). Clearly, for Hertzberg, as for Ridout, Saul functions negatively, as a paradigm, an example of failure to respond properly to the demands of God, and positively, as a pointer towards a model of obedient response, of a proper relationship with God.

Still, there is more to Hertzberg's evaluation than this. For, like many before him (as in the extract from Hastings, above, and, as already remarked, more noticeably so in Jewish tradition),[3] he is prepared to recognize, indeed to paint in strong colours, some positive qualities in Saul: "he is pious in the extreme, brave yet modest, without doubt a man of the stuff of which kings are made". These are stirring words. What function do they have in Hertzberg's evaluation of the king? On the one hand, of course, they make the theological point about Saul's failure so much the sharper. Saul was all these things yet he did not measure up to the demands of God - for in themselves these things were insufficient. On the other hand, such praise of Saul softens

the judgement; no man like this can have been a <u>total</u>
failure. Saul demands our sympathy. Thus it is not altogether surprising that Hertzberg's closing comments on
the story of Saul (p. 234) include a description of Saul's life
as "a life full of tragic greatness".

Saul is a model of human failure; he is also a figure of
tragedy, a figure who prompts sorrow. Accounts of the
story of Saul in such terms are many. For present purposes
let me instance just a few. The first is from Hastings (p. 63):

It is one of the many signs of the reality and
truthfulness of Scripture history, that the examples
most held up for our warning are not those of the
worst men, but those of persons in whom there has
been a doubtful conflict between good and evil, and
the evil has ultimately prevailed; or of men who,
having been placed in the midst of high privileges and
responsibilities, have fallen back on their ordinary
characters and natural enjoyments, and despised their
loftier calling. To the latter of these classes belongs
Esau, whose character is referred to in the Epistle to
the Hebrews for our avoidance; to the former belongs
Saul, the first king of Israel. As if to throw a
stronger light on the character of the unhappy Saul
by comparison or contrast, the Scriptures present him
along with Samuel, the man of prayer, with David,
the man after God's own heart, with his son Jonathan,
so lovely yet so truly great. Saul might have prayed
like Samuel, might have waited upon God as David
did, might have loved with largeness of heart like
Jonathan. But his story is the story of the downward
progress of the soul; his life is a succession of gradual
changes, and in his successive trials evil prevails over
the spirit of grace and opportunities of good. As a
day that begins with sunshine and then clouds over
gloomily and at last closes with a storm, so is the life
of Saul. He is the most tragic character in the Old
Testament records; historically tragic in the solitary
awfulness of his might and the unutterable pathos of
his fall; yet more ethically tragic, a soul of noblest
endowments and highest aspirations struggling against and overborne by surroundings, duties, claims,
to which his nature was unequal. It is the theme of

the old Greek tragedians; they lay it on an irresistible, cruel, overruling Fate. It is the theme of Shakespeare; he bares the springs of moral and mental weakness causing it. It is the theme of the Hebrew historian; he sees in it the contest between a good and evil spirit from the Lord.

This is an interesting passage, for its simple exposition of these two ingredients in the evaluation of the story of Saul - exemplary failure and tragedy - also conveniently exposes some difficulties with the evaluation itself. Central to the tradition of viewing Saul as a model of failure is, of course, an account of his weakness or sin. This is perhaps most often spoken of in terms of his "disobedience" although there have been many ways of exploring in detail this "fault" (as we shall see shortly). My point here is that such an interpretation of the Saul story is congenial to one particular kind of tragedy, that in which the tragic hero is depicted as "flawed" in some way - the kind of tragedy which Hastings, rightly or wrongly, typifies as Shakespearian, where the author "bares the springs of moral and mental weakness causing [the hero's fall]". On the other hand, we might wonder what place "character flaw" has in a drama where the hero's fall is due to "an irresistible, cruel, overruling Fate"? Hastings speaks in this connection of Aeschylus and Sophocles. Is Oedipus (in Sophocles' play) to be condemned for his behaviour, held up as an exemplar of moral or religious failure? On most readings of the play I should have thought that the answer was "no".[4] The tragedy of Oedipus is what we might call a tragedy of Fate rather than a tragedy of Flaw. The question then is, what sort of a tragedy is the tragedy of King Saul? Curiously Hastings, whether intentionally or not, seems to suggest that it is a tragedy of Fate, for the Hebrew author, he says, sees the hero's fall in terms of a "contest between a good and evil spirit from the Lord". That is to say, it is the god (Fate?) who controls the forces which dictate the hero's fortunes. Such is Gloster's view of the tragic experience:

As flies to wanton boys are we to the gods,
They kill us for their sport. [King Lear, IV,ii]

The same tension - between the interpretation which

sees the hero as flawed and thus creating his own fate, and that which sees him in the grip of forces or circumstances beyond his control - is apparent in my second example of a "tragic" interpretation. Von Rad observes (1965:324f.) that

> to faith [Saul's] supreme interest was as the anointed who slipped from Jahweh's hand, the one quitting the stage, and yielding to him who was coming; that is, Saul as the God-forsaken, driven from one delusion to the other, desperate, and in the end swallowed up in miserable darkness. Right to the end the stories follow the unhappy king on his way with a deep human sympathy, and unfold a tragedy which in its final act rises to solemn grandeur. Actually, Israel never again gave birth to a poetic [i.e. literary] production which in certain of its features has such close affinity with the spirit of Greek tragedy. However convinced the story-tellers are of Saul's guilt, still there is at the same time something supra-personal in the way in which he became guilty - it is the fate which overtakes the one from whom God had turned away....Of course, Saul was not in the power of a dark destiny, nor had he overreached himself in hybris. He was called to be a special tool of the will of Jahweh in history, for it was through him that Jahweh wanted to give effect to his plan to save Israel (I Sam. IX.16). On this task he came to disaster.

There is unresolved tension in this analysis too. Von Rad wants to assert Saul's "guilt", yet he cannot but admit that "there is...something supra-personal in the way in which he became guilty". The passage is full of phrases which indicate a reading of the "failure" as beyond Saul's control: Saul is the "God-forsaken" and the fate which "overtakes" him follows from the fact that "God had turned away"; he is "driven" from one delusion to another - by whom?, we want to ask. Perhaps realizing the fragility of his position von Rad hastens to back away from this interesting parallel with Greek tragedy by denying any essential similarity between the causes of Saul's downfall and those typical of Greek tragic heroes - "of course" Saul's sin is not "hybris" (man over-reaching himself, overweaning ambition), nor is he in the power of some dark destiny (cf. Hastings!). Yet what then is this "supra-personal" dimension to "the way in which he became guilty"? Given the limited number of characters in the story can this be anything other than some dimension of God? I find it fascinating that von Rad moves directly from denying that Saul was in the grip of a dark power to affirming that he was, rather, "called to be a special tool of the will of Jahweh". A tool of Yahweh? A "supra-personal" dimension to his "guilt"? The clear implication seems to be that in some way this is a tragedy of Fate and that the supra-personal agency with the hero in its grip is none other than God (Yahweh). But although this is the logical implication of his analysis von Rad will not allow that on this reading perhaps the "blame" for Saul's fall cannot be pinned upon Saul himself but must lie ultimately with God. In that case might we not affirm rather than deny that Saul is depicted as being in the power of a "dark destiny"? For again the logic of this analysis of the story as a tragedy of Fate, is that in this context Yahweh functions as Fate itself, as the "dark destiny" which holds sway over the king.

The same tension, between fate and flaw, can be met frequently in exposition of the King Saul story as tragedy. Our final example is in two brief extracts (pp. 78f.) from Welch's fine essay on Saul:

> And Saul went down to meet his end, a great soul face to face with a ravelled world who refuses to turn his back on what he has taken upon him, but also a great soul with a fatal defect in his nature, not quite big enough to do the thing which his time demanded from its leader, but doing all which it was left possible for him to do.

> But here is a man, all a man, wrestling with fate and with the dark powers which hem in every man's destiny, which limit him at every point in his effort to reach the thing he has set before him.

Again we have, set out with clarity, both elements in the analysis - the tragic flaw and the hostility of fate. Again we may ask, so what ultimately is the cause of Saul's fall? Is it "flaw" or is it the machinations of these "dark powers"? If, as the commentators wish to assert, it is somehow both (von Rad: "However convinced the story-tellers are of

Saul's guilt, <u>still there is at the same time</u> something supra-personal in the way in which he became guilty"), then clearly there is need for some explanation of the "some-how", a need to look more closely at the alleged "causes" and to clarify how they stand in relation to each other.[5] Any moral or theological evaluation of the story must hinge on this question of the cause or causes of the fall; for if the sole or primary cause is Saul's own weakness then obviously he may properly be deemed culpable (and so provide a fitting exemplar of moral or religious failure), but if some dimension of Fate (Yahweh?) is primary, so much the less may Saul be deemed blameworthy, whatever his character defects, and so much the more must the motivation (and so nature of God as he appears in the story), be opened to question.

Logically speaking the tragedy of Fate and the tragedy of the character flaw are incompatible. Aesthetically speaking they are not, as may be observed in practice. Scott Fitzgerald once observed that an artist is one who can hold two irreconcilable views together and still function, and I would suggest that this is not a bad definition of the thought-world of many a work of art. Shakespeare's Macbeth has, as we shall later observe, some interesting points in common with the story of King Saul, and, while not prejudicing whether this is one of them, it may be noted here that it is a play which contains elements of both tragic causes: it is common to ascribe Macbeth's fall to his fatal flaw, ambition; but I have also seen a most convincing production in the "Greek" style, with Macbeth from the beginning in the grip of a Fate which manifests itself and controls him, at the most obvious level, through the witches. It is in the nature of much literature of high seriousness to thrive on an ambiguity which challenges the reader to wrestle with the meaning and which reflects the ambiguity of life. With that sobering thought in mind I do not pretend that we shall find any definitive answers to our question about these key elements in any interpretation of the story of Saul. But perhaps we can hope to see some of the possibilities of interpretation more clearly.

Chapter Two
SAUL'S FAILURE: 1 SAMUEL 13

The formal rejection of Saul by God takes place in chapters 13 and 15. If we are to look for some weakness in Saul, some general flaw or specific sin which might be said to be the cause of his fall, these chapters seem an obvious starting point. Why did God reject Saul? At least a prima facie answer is likely to be found here. Let us start, then, with chapter 13.

Saul has defeated the Ammonites at Jabesh-Gilead and been confirmed in his new role as king. But the Philistines are still a threat. Provoked by Jonathan's defeat of their forces at Geba (13:3f.) the Philistines gather for a major onslaught. Saul calls up the men of Israel to Gilgal but faced with the huge Philistine army the people begin to desert him. Saul has been instructed by Samuel (10:8) to wait seven days at Gilgal until he, Samuel, should come and offer sacrifice. Having waited seven days, Saul feels constrained to offer the sacrifice himself (verses 8f.):

> He waited seven days, the time appointed by Samuel; but Samuel did not come to Gilgal, and the people were scattering from him. So Saul said, "Bring the burnt offering here to me, and the peace offerings". And he offered the burnt offering.

Immediately Samuel appears and condemns him (verse 13).

> "You have done foolishly; you have not kept the commandment of Yahweh your God, which he commanded you".

What is Saul's crime? Commentators have long been in

33

difficulties over this question and have come up with various answers. Obviously the first step to take is to identify the commandment which Saul has broken, and this seems relatively straightforward. If it is a particular command then it is most naturally connected with Samuel's instruction to Saul in 10:8, after their first meeting and Saul's designation as future king:

"And you shall go down before me to Gilgal; and behold, I am coming to you to offer burnt offerings and to sacrifice peace offerings. Seven days you shall wait, until I come to you and show you what you shall do".

Here in chapter 13 we have Saul, in Gilgal, waiting seven days, "the time appointed by Samuel", and then himself, reluctantly,[1] offering sacrifices. Samuel, as prophet, speaks the word of Yahweh; that he should speak here of his command to wait as "the commandment of Yahweh" appears a natural enough transition. The alternative to taking "commandment" with this particular reference is to construe it as referring to some general law which Saul has broken by himself offering the sacrifice, the most likely being a law which prohibited any but a priest from officiating at the sacrifice. Both interpretations of "commandment" have had and still have their advocates, and, indeed, it is possible to argue that both are operative at once.

If the commandment which was broken was the particular instruction to wait the seven days until Samuel would come to offer sacrifice then the sin was that of disobedience to the prophet, and hence to the word of Yahweh. If the commandment was a general one governing cultic practice then the sin was perhaps the fact that Saul wrongly intruded on the priestly office (taking Samuel in the role of priest as well as prophet) or, as some modern commentators speculate, in some (now unknown) way he misperformed the sacrifice that was appropriate before a "holy war" (as these scholars designate it). A third understanding is that the instruction was itself framed to protect Saul from breaking a cultic law and so his sin was both the cultic one and disobedience to the particular command to wait for Samuel.

Are there any clues to a solution? Looking outside the

passage, advocates of the view that Saul had broken a cultic
law sometimes point to 2 Chron 26:16-21 where king Uzziah
(Azariah) was condemned for entry into the temple to burn
incense; but against this is the problem that the evidence
here comes from a much later source, Chronicles, and that
elsewhere in the Deuteronomistic History (in the books of
Samuel and Kings) we are given no reason to suppose that
there was any absolute prohibition against a king performing
sacrificial rites (and cf. 1 Sam 14:33-35, 2 Sam 8:18, 20:26, 1
Kings 3:3). As regards "holy war": the notion is a
problematic one and I shall look a little more closely at it in
connection with chapter 15 (below, Chapter 3) where it has
at least some prima facie claim to be considered a pertinent
factor. In the present context let it suffice to say that if
there is little enough evidence to prove that in monarchical
Israel some wars were especially designated "holy" and
others not, according to some well-known institution, there
is considerably less that the war spoken of in chapter 13 was
so conceived in our story.[2] Moreover, as Smith remarks
(p. 98), if the rejection were a matter of Saul's usurpation of
the priestly office it is strange that the narrator gives no
indication whatsoever of such usurpation anywhere in the
story, either here in chapter 13 or elsewhere. It is certainly
difficult to sustain as the best interpretation[3]. The
reason it has been sought as an explanation is simple:
commentators have been puzzled by the fact that if the
commandment is taken, as in the broader context it is most
readily taken, to be the instruction to wait (10:8), then on at
least one reading of the close context Saul appears to have
fulfilled the letter if not the spirit of the instruction - he is
said in verse 8 to have "waited seven days, the time
appointed by Samuel", and in verse 11 he protests that "you
did not come within the days appointed".

The way out of the difficulty, however, is not, in my
view, to seek an explanation outside the terms of the text in
some unattested cultic law but to work through the
information that we do have in the text. Conventionally
there are two routes taken. The first is to assume that
since Samuel condemns Saul, the king must not in fact have
fulfilled the conditions of the instruction, despite the
apparent implication of verses 8 and 11. Thus, for example,
after the fashion of much Jewish exegesis David Kimchi

(commentary on 13:9) explains that Saul should have waited till the night, instead of just the morning, of the seventh day; by contrast the "fire and brimstone" tradition of Protestant Christianity is generally reluctant to enter into such detail on the question, but, being anxious to move to more important concerns such as the condemnation of Saul and to expatiate on the king's sinful nature, simply indicate that the set time was "nearly expired" (Robinson, 28; Hastings, 73) or leave the whole matter of how precisely the instruction was broken decently obscure (cf. Wilberforce, 218). Nor, for that matter, do modern "critical" commentators who assume the breaking of the instruction often attempt to clarify the point.

Another response is to take the narrator's sentence in verse 8 and Saul's protest in verse 11 at their face value. The instruction said to wait seven days; the narrator tells us in verse 8 that Saul waited seven days; and Saul himself is depicted protesting as much in verse 11. Thus Smith (p. 98), Mauchline (p. 113f.) and Hertzberg (p. 105f.) comment, respectively:[4]

> It is difficult to discover anything in the text at which Samuel could justly take offence. The original command was to wait seven days, and this Saul did. In the circumstances he might well plead that he had been too scrupulous. It would not be impertinent to ask why Samuel had waited so long before appearing.

> Saul seems to come well out of the incident. Samuel's riposte sounds unconvincing to us (vss. 13-14)....Which commandment is not specified; we may feel convinced that [Samuel's] reference is to his own instruction to Saul to wait for him (10:8), but that had been obeyed within the limit set by Samuel himself....The impression left on the reader unquestionably is that the sentence was unfair and against the evidence.

> Saul...justifies his conduct in a modest and at all points irrefutable way. From the description of the affair we seem to have a vindication of Saul rather than a charge aganst him. Saul had done what was permissable for him to do according to Samuel's express instructions....If anyone is in the wrong here it is Samuel and not Saul.

What then is Saul's "fault"? Mauchline takes the matter no further. Smith and Hertzberg, however, have more to add.

Hertzberg - we shall come back to Smith in due course - feels sure that, taking the overall picture of Saul and Samuel in the story of Saul as a whole it is the compiler's intention to show that Saul had trespassed from the beginning of his kingship. Therefore, despite the fact that the "proper content of the material" depicts Saul sympathetically it was felt nevertheless by the redactor to be capable of reflecting disapproval of the king. Thus Hertzberg writes (p. 106) of the passage that in it we see "a manifest contradiction between the proper content of the material used and the purpose for which the compiler wanted to use it". By the compiler Saul's trespass is seen as consisting in the fact that he did not act according to the spirit of the instruction: that is, whatever the precise instruction (seven days or whatever) the important thing for one who was truly and utterly "obedient" would have been to wait until Samuel, the prophet of God, came to give further lead.

Thus on this view (Hertzberg, 106),

[Saul] had no patience, i.e. no faith, and allowed the disturbing situation to be the most important factor in his decision.

On this view (that of Hertzberg's "compiler") the offence is less strictly disobedience than an underlying lack of faith.[5] Blaikie (pp. 211f.) puts it more strongly:

Saul was under instructions to wait seven days at Gilgal, at the end, if not before the end, of which time Samuel promised to come to him. This was a distinct instruction from Samuel, God's known and recognized prophet, acting in God's name and with a view to obtaining of God's countenance and guidance in the awful crisis of the nation....The real offence of Saul was that he disregarded the absence of God's prophet and representative, of the man who had all along been the mediator between God and the king and between God and the people. If Saul had had a real conviction that all depended at this moment on his getting God's help...he would not have acted as if

Samuel's presence was of no moment....God was not a reality to Saul.

For me the problem with Hertzberg's approach is that he is prepared too readily to abandon the impression which the passage actually leaves on him in favour of what he thinks that impression ought to be (in the light of other material in the Saul story), without reconsidering the whole picture. Since the sympathetic depiction of Saul and the problem of the hard-to-find fault will not easily go away his solution is, for all practical purposes, to ignore this passage in his reading of the Saul story. But before I take such a drastic step I should wish to explore further whether the undoubted tension exposed through this scene has an integral place in the wider story. Hertzberg dismisses his own exegesis because it does not fit with his picture of the rest of the work. I am curious to see what happens to the picture of the rest of the work if a sympathetic exegesis of Saul in this scene is allowed to be a factor in the formulation of that wider picture.

In point of fact, it could be argued that if the rest of the story be considered for a moment the picture is not obviously as Hertzberg paints it. The attempt to lay at Saul's door the fault of "lack of faith" is one that runs counter to much evidence elsewhere (in our story) of Saul as a pious man, devoted to Yahweh (as is recognized by Hertzberg himself, p. 133): he is ever anxious (perhaps over-anxious) to perform his religious duties - and gets himself into difficulties thereby, in chapter 14 as well as in chapter 13 - and, remarkably, remains throughout his life absolutely loyal in his religious commitment to Yahweh alone amongst gods.[6] To be sure, the ascription to Saul of "lack of faith" could be argued to gain some support from 15:22f. (the second "rejection" episode) as we shall see, in which case the many expressions of Saul's piety have to be taken (as is frequently done by commentators though more often by default than design) as in some way defective and superficial, a matter of "mere" piety rather than "faith", outward form rather that inward disposition. What I would suggest, however, is that if such an explanation is to be brought to bear upon the problems of chapter 13 it must be considered very much an explanation of last resort.

Is there another way forward which takes seriously the "sympathetic" portrayal of Saul and yet recognizes the earnestness of Samuel's accusation and condemnation? I believe that there is and that Blaikie is touching on it when he sets out his understanding of what it is that Saul is instructed to do. The instruction in 10:8 is as follows:

"And you shall go down before me to Gilgal; and behold, I am coming to you to offer burnt offerings and to sacrifice peace offerings. Seven days you shall wait, until I come to you and show you what you shall do".

Blaikie (p. 211) paraphrases this as:

Samuel was under instructions to wait seven days at Gilgal, at the end, if not before the end, of which time Samuel promised to come to him.

This way of putting it suggests that the seven days are merely an approximate indication of the time that Saul should allow to elapse before expecting Samuel; the heart of the instruction is not in the "seven days" but in the coming of Samuel (and his showing Saul what to do). Saul (and so too Mauchline, Smith and Hertzberg!) take the instruction as essentially entailing a prohibition against taking any action until seven days have elapsed, for until that period has elapsed Samuel is to be expected: "seven days you shall wait". Samuel (and so, for example, Blaikie), on the other hand, sees himself as commanding Saul to wait about seven days until he [Samuel] should come:

"...you shall wait until I come to you and show you what you shall do".

Here is the point. The instruction to "wait" is ambiguous with regard to time. On Samuel's interpretation Saul has not waited as instructed, for he should have waited until the prophet came and issued further instructions; as Saul sees it he has waited precisely the required time, seven days, before being at liberty to take action himself.

Smith (p. 98), who sees the instruction as Saul sees it, concludes that the condemnation is arbitrary:

The only conclusion to which we can come is that the author glorifies the sovereign will of Yahweh who

rejects and chooses according to his own good
pleasure. Samuel is the embodiment of this sovereign
will.

My own suggestion, that the instruction can be seen both
ways, leads easily to the same conclusion. But what appears
arbitrary about the condemnation, where we see the
excercise of Yahweh's will "according to his own good
pleasure", is not, as Smith suggests, that the judgement is
perverse, in simple defiance of the clear meaning of the
command in question, but rather that Yahweh, though
Samuel, requires of Saul "this" rather than "that" interpretation. I shall come back to this point in due course.

I suggest, therefore, that a provisional answer to the
question, Why (in chapter 13) does God reject Saul?, can be
given as follows. The immediate cause appears to be Saul's
breaking of Samuel's instruction in 10:8. But we have seen
that this instruction is ambiguous and that on Saul's
understanding no sin has been committed. The question
therefore resolves itself into one about the motives of
Samuel and Yahweh. Why is no account taken of Saul's
defence? Is Samuel unaware of the ambiguity of the
instruction or does he choose to ignore it? Does the real
cause of Saul's rejection lie, not in his action in chapter 13,
but in the attitude of Yahweh towards him, or perhaps
something he represents?

Chapter Three
SAUL'S FAILURE: 1 SAMUEL 15

Samuel comes to Saul with a command from Yahweh. Saul is to attack the Amalekites and devote to God, by destroying ("put to the ban", "utterly destroy" - hrm), them and all that is theirs. In due course Saul defeats the Amalekites (15:8f.):

> And he took Agag the king of the Amalekites alive, and utterly destroyed (hrm) all the people with the edge of the sword. But Saul and the people spared Agag, and the best of the sheep and of the oxen and of the fatlings, and the lambs, and all that was good, and would not utterly destroy them (hrm); all that was despised and worthless they utterly destroyed (hrm).

Yahweh sends word to Samuel (verse 11):

> "I repent that I have made Saul king; for he has turned back from following me, and has not performed my commandments".

Samuel is told that Saul has gone to Gilgal, so he meets him there, and accuses him of disobeying Yahweh's command (verse 19):

> "Why did you swoop on the spoil, and do what was evil in the sight of Yahweh?"

Saul protests that, on the contrary, he has done what was asked of him (verses 20f.):

> "I have obeyed the voice of Yahweh, I have gone on the mission on which Yahweh sent me, I have brought

41

Agag the king of Amalek, and I have utterly destroyed (hrm) the Amalekites. And the people took
of the spoil, sheep and oxen, the best of the things
devoted to destruction (hrm), to sacrifice to Yahweh
your God in Gilgal".

Samuel retorts with those much quoted lines (verses 22f.):

"Has Yahweh as great delight in burnt offerings
　　and sacrifices,
　　as in obeying the voice of Yahweh?
Behold, to obey is better than sacrifice,
　　and to hearken than the fat of rams".

He goes on to declare that because Saul has rejected the
word of Yahweh, so Yahweh has rejected him from being
king. Saul then acknowledges that he has sinned:

"for I have transgressed the commandment of
Yahweh and your words, because I feared the people
and obeyed their voice".

His request for pardon, in order that he might again worship
God with Samuel, is thrown back at him and he is told that
Yahweh has rejected him and given the kingdom to a
"neighbour". A final plea by Saul that he be allowed to
worship God with Samuel before the people is this time
acceded to. Saul worships Yahweh while Samuel hews Agag
in pieces before Yahweh. Samuel and Saul go to their
respective homes.
　　Unlike in chapter 13, commentators generally find in this
chapter no difficulty in determining Saul's "fault". He was
commanded to destroy utterly ("put to the ban") the
Amalekites "to the last chicken" (Good, 69). He fails to do
so, and in the view of many critics, compounds his sin, his
failure to obey to the letter God's word, by hypocritically
pretending that he had done what was required (verses 13,
20), and by attempting to put the blame for his failure on
the people (verses 15, 24). If opprobrium is to be heaped on
Saul then chapter 15 usually provides the occasion par
excellence (Robinson, 49, and Blaikie, 252f., respectively):

What wonder was it then, that the Lord rejected him,
whose best service was an act of vile dissimulation?

Saul's Failure: 1 Samuel 15

We read not, that he was ever humbled for his offence. Though he was spared for a long time after this transaction, the goodness of God did not lead him to repentance; for he continued, to the last, proud, and cruel, and profane.

Saul's worst qualities had now become petrified. His wilfulness, his selfishness, his passionateness, his jealousy, had now got complete control, nor could their current be turned aside. The threat of losing his kingdom - perhaps the most terrible threat such a man could have felt - had failed to turn him from his wayward course. He was like the man in the iron cage in "Pilgrim's Progress", who gave his history: "I left off to watch and be sober; I sinned against the light of the word and goodness of God; I have grieved the Spirit and He is gone; I tempted the devil, and he is come to me; I have provoked God to anger and He has left me; I have so hardened my heart that I cannot repent". It is a terrible lesson that comes to us from the career of Saul. If our natural lusts are not under the restraint of a higher power; if by that power we are not trained to watch, and check, and overpower them, if we allow them to burst all restraint and lord it over us as they will, - then will they grow into so many tyrants, who will rule us with rods of iron; laugh at the feeble remonstrances of our conscience; scoff at every messenger of God, vex His Holy Spirit, and hurl us at last to everlasting woe!

A little startled, I search again through the pages of my · Bible. Was it such a monstrous sin? Have I missed something? I am reassured (Chappell, 134):

Saul did sin. He sinned deeply. But there have been countless others who sinned in a far more ugly and hideous way than he whose lives yet ended in glory and in victory. Saul was never so guilty of any sin · half so detestable as the sin of his successor, who came to be a man after God's own heart. The · tragedy of the life of Saul was not so much in the fact that he sinned as in the fact that he could never be brought to face his sin and to confess it and to hate it and to put it away.

43

Now this is interesting. This commentator is so far from recognizing anything particularly heinous in Saul's sin, that he is obliged to locate the king's tragic flaw elsewhere, in a supposed inability to repent. It is not the validity of the "insincerity" interpretation that need detain us here; it has been argued by others (for example, Hertzberg, 76) but faces difficulties in coping with Saul's expressed repentence in verses 24-5 and the fact that the rejection (in verse 23) is tied specifically to the matter of the disobedience, not to any question of repentance. Rather, what is of interest is the tacit acknowledgement that there is some imbalance between the "sin" and the "punishment".

Chappell is not alone in sensing an imbalance. While others are content to find the cause of rejection in the act of disobedience, the sparing of Agag and part of the spoil, they are often at pains to stress the alleged hypocrisy of Saul or his perfidy in shifting the blame upon the people, as though this particular crime of disobedience were hardly enough to warrant the sentence which follows upon it. Sometimes, indeed, the expression of doubt about the relationship between sin and sentence is more explicit. Knierim, for example, questions (p. 36) conventional explanations of the sin in terms of the infringement of cultic law or the opposition of two types of religion (those of prophet and priest). Do such explanations

> really explain the radicality of the judgement of rejection? Even David himself had become guilty of the violation of central and sacral laws (II Sam., chs. 11f. and 24) without having been rejected.

Soggin (p. 195) is blunter:

> To the modern reader Saul might hardly seem to be a "sinner", and we might doubt whether his "sin" made much impression on the reader or hearer of that time.

Clearly, then, this story of Saul and the Amalekites bears closer examination. What precisely is the accusation against him? How culpable is he?

As already observed, most commentators speak of his failure here in terms of disobedience. After all, this is precisely what Samuel accuses him of: "Why then did you not obey the word of Yahweh?...You have rejected the word of Yahweh". For many it is the simple _fact_ of disobedience that constitutes the sin. For others, however, there is also involved the question of what the broken commandment was about, and to me also, this seems to be an important question. While it is conceivable that, in terms of the story, the act of disobedience _is_ all that counts, it is also possible that the picture being painted is not just in black and white, not just a matter of "goodies" and "baddies" but of complex characters and conflicting moral and theological elements.

Saul is commanded to ḥrm the Amalekites. What does this mean? The word ḥrm seems to be connected with the idea of holiness, separation or taboo and can be used of various things forbidden to common use. In the Old Testament it is especially connected with warfare and the status of a defeated enemy and his possessions, and is used in some texts of the extermination of an enemy and the destruction of booty. In scholarly theory the term is often connected with the "holy war", a concept which owes much to the advocacy of von Rad's book (1951). He argued that "holy war" was a homogeneous and distinct institution in ancient Israel with a number of recognizable features. These he drew piecemeal from various biblical contexts to form a theoretical reconstruction of the original institution (idea). But despite the attractiveness of the theory for supplying a background to some biblical texts and the support it has sometimes been found to have in analogies with the Islamic jihad, it remains very much a notional matter as the criticisms of recent scholars make clear.[1] In essence the problem lies, as Gottwald (1976:942) observes, in "the high incidence of erratic and contradictory war practices [instanced in the Old Testament]":

This strongly indicates that the entire range of traits compiled by von Rad was never normative in Israel. Steps toward initiating holy war, for example, which von Rad viewed as serial and cumulative, may in fact have been alternative courses followed on different occasions....Even more tellingly, the different accounts of the destruction of war captives and booty, or of their reservation or setting aside for sacred use, show great variation from the schematic formulations of the later Deuteronomistic program of ḥerem.... What is in question, therefore, is not the existence, but the frequency, scope, and degree of standardization of holy-war practices.

It is clear, then, that despite the confidence with which some scholars have spoken of the "holy war" it is a concept which is clothed in considerable uncertainty. Nor does our present text do much to clarify matters. Nowhere is reference made to any special condition distinguishing this war from any other except that a specific stipulation is made by the prophet concerning the disposal of the "booty". When the prophet accuses Saul of disobeying the word of Yahweh he nowhere suggests that Saul has broken some well-known cultic law relating to some well-known and distinctive category of war. On the contrary he simply asserts that Saul has not completely fulfilled the specific instruction regarding the spoil. That "holy war" was a concept important to our narrative is a moot point.

If "holy war" is thus an uncertain base on which to build an understanding of the precise nature of Saul's crime, perhaps the term ḥrm (which does have the advantage of being securely located in our text) will avail us more. We have seen that linguistic evidence suggests a meaning of something like "to devote to a god by destruction". Clearly, then, it is something akin to the notion of "sacrifice" (zbḥ). Now this last observation is, I believe, of fundamental importance for understanding this chapter. Let me turn to our text for a closer examination, and I trust my point may become apparent.

In verse 3, Samuel, speaking formally as the messenger of Yahweh, demands that all Amalek be ḥrm, and the subsequent clauses in apposition - "do not spare [have compassion on] them, but kill both man and woman," etc. - make absolutely clear that ḥrm means destruction. Saul duly attacks and defeats the Āmalekites. But then in verse 9 we read of the sparing of Agag and the best of the spoil. As if to doubly underline the apparent disregard of the prophet's command the narrator repeats the key terms of the commandment: "Saul and the people spared Agag and the best of the [spoil]...and would not destroy (ḥrm) them". And to make matters worse, the account of the sparing ends by emphasizing the fact that what was spared was the best of the spoil; only what was despised and worthless was devoted to destruction (ḥrm).

Saul's Failure: 1 Samuel 15

On the face of it this action can only be seen to be in defiance of Yahweh, and indeed Yahweh is depicted as taking it to be so (verses 10f.). He anounces to Samuel his "repentance" (nhm) of having chosen Saul; accordingly next morning Samuel arrives, angry, at Gilgal to meet Saul.

There is great subtlety in the writing here. The black shadow already cast over Saul extends further: Samuel is told of Saul, that "he came to Carmel, and behold, he set up[2] a monument to himself". Then on meeting Samuel at Gilgal Saul greets him with what to the reader at this stage in the proceedings is a most astonishing sentence:

"Blessed be you to Yahweh: I have performed Yahweh's commandment".

The retort of the older commentators was "dissimulation!". Indeed, it looks as though a self-regarding Saul, not content with failing to fulfil the command, is now trying to deceive the prophet. His predicament worsens. Samuel observes coldly:

"What then is this bleating of the sheep in my ears, and the lowing of oxen which I hear?"

Then comes a remarkable and dramatic shift in Saul's favour. The king replies, apparently without embarassment, by volunteering the information that the noise issues from the best of the Amalekite livestock which has been brought here - to sacrifice to Yahweh. Now we have a completely different view of what is going on: to be sure, Saul and the people had not "devoted to destruction" the best of the livestock on the spot, at the scene of battle (or wherever), but that was because they had decided it would be more appropriate to "devote" it to Yahweh at his own sanctuary. Seen in this light, of course, the sparing of the best of the spoil makes excellent sense, for how could they bring what was despised and worthless back to Gilgal to sacrifice formally to their God?

Curiously - or should we say characteristically? - Samuel wishes to hear nothing more: "Stop! I will tell you what Yahweh said to me this night". To which the narrator has Saul - by now growing accustomed to this kind of scene? - reply simply, "Say on". With sarcasm ("Though you are little in your own eyes")[3] Samuel sets out his accusation:

47

"Why then did you not obey the voice of Yahweh? Why did you swoop on the spoil, and do what was evil in the sight of Yahweh?"

· Then comes what I think is the key to the scene. Saul replies, again unabashed:

"I have obeyed the voice of Yahweh: I have gone on the mission which Yahweh sent me, I have brought Agag the king of Amalek, and I have devoted to destruction the Amalekites; and[4] the people have taken of the spoil, sheep and oxen, the best of the things devoted to destruction, to sacrifice to Yahweh your god in Gilgal".

This is a splendidly forthright reply. As in the earlier speech, much of which is simply reiterated (with perhaps a strong note of irritation), there is no evasion of the pertinent "facts". Saul freely acknowledges that Agag is present at Gilgal and that the people have brought the best of the spoil to Gilgal. Saul asserts, however, that these facts are consonant with his fulfilment of the prophet's instruction. Now had they been so patently in contravention of the instruction we might have expected the king to veil them in some way (by claiming, perhaps, that the livestock were captured elsewhere, and so on). On the contrary, Saul's response makes clear (what the first response suggested) that it is not the "facts" that are in dispute but their interpretation vis-à-vis the instruction. There is ambiguity in Saul's reply only with regard to one item, namely his intentions concerning Agag. This matter apart the reply appears as unanswerable a justification as the earlier report (verse 9) seemed a condemnation. Has Yahweh moved too hastily? Agag apart (and we shally come back to him shortly), when the best of the livestock has been sacrificed the devotion to destruction of all Amalek will be complete. There was nothing in Yahweh's command about the precise circumstances of the destruction; so the people had wished to pay special honour to Yahweh at the same time as fulfilling his command, and Saul had acquiesced.

But questions arise. Is it true that there was nothing about the precise circumstances of the destruction in Yahweh's command? What if hrm should plainly mean "to destroy on the spot"? From the reaction of both Yahweh and Samuel it would seem that, strictly speaking, hrm is not compatible with zbh (sacrifice); despite Saul's explanation Samuel goes on specifically to contrast obedience and sacrifice - a contrast which only makes sense if we assume that to bring the spoil to sacrifice at Gilgal could not count, for Samuel at least, as fulfilling the instruction to "devote to destruction". Whether the key to the technical incompatibility of hrm and zbh lay in where the destruction took place or in some specific cultic rites to be observed, or in both, we simply do not know. But while it would help us to be a little more "at home" with the story were we to have this detailed background knowledge, it is not, I believe, fundamentally important for our understanding of the text. This supplies sufficient information without such detail.

The fact is that, as the story has it, neither Saul nor the people were aware that there was any significant incompatibility; neither realized that to bring to a sanctuary livestock designated hrm in order to offer it to God as a sacrifice (zbh) was to infringe seriously the rules of hrm (or zbh, or both). If we suppose them to have been thus aware then their action in so risking divine wrath becomes particularly difficult to comprehend, since all they were attempting to do was to honour Yahweh by their action. Gilgal figures prominently in the story of Saul as above all the place where the people meet in assembly and where they offer sacrifice to Yahweh; so what could be more natural than that the returning army should wish to share the major sacrifice with the whole community before their God in his central sanctuary?

Many a commentator has labelled Saul as "greedy" - greedy because it is accepted (as, to be sure, the narrator leads us to accept in verse 9) that the spoil was spared for his and the people's own personal enrichment - assuming his "hypocrisy" and "dissimulation" in verses 13ff. (cf. Robinson, 45, 49f., Wilberforce, 221, and Blaikie, 248) without second thought.[5] Why, on the contrary, should we (or Samuel) believe that Saul's explanation is genuine? The answer is to reiterate the point already made about that final phrase of Saul's explanation (verse 21), "in Gilgal". Why else should Saul and the people have come to Gilgal, the sanctuary of Yahweh, the scene of sacrifice, if not to do precisely what he claims?

And this assumption of Saul's sincerity is no modern invention: the LXX actually reads, at the end of verse 12:

> And he [Samuel] came down to Gilgal to Saul, and behold he [Saul] offered a burnt offering to Yahweh, the firstfruits of the spoil which be brought from Amalek.[6]

Whether the reading is original or a later expansion does not matter greatly; either way it lends powerful support to our exegesis and encourages us to take Saul's explanation as offered in good faith, as we have seen the context to suggest.

Thus if Samuel's bitter contrast between obedience and sacrifice only makes sense when it is assumed that he saw a significant incompatibility between "devotion" (ḥrm) and "sacrifice" (zbḥ) of the booty, so Saul's (and the people's) actions and subsequent protestations that the command had been fulfilled only make sense when it is assumed that they, for their part, saw no significant incompatibility.

But there is an outstanding question mark in Saul's explanation to Samuel. What about Agag? Was Saul intending to put him to death here, "before Yahweh at Gilgal", thus truly completing the ḥrm of all Amalek, or was he, in fact, going to spare him, and in this respect, at least, break the terms of the commandment? We are not told directly. We do not know for sure. But while the storyteller opens up the tantalizing possibility that after all Saul had acted not wholly in good faith he allows us at the same time no confidence in this possibility. It is not easy to see how, without a positive hint that Agag was to be exempted from the fate of the rest of Amalek, we can set this particular element of Saul's action against the strong impression of sincerity that we have otherwise found in his response. More specifically, there may perhaps be found a hint of Saul's intention in the way in which his reference (verse 20) to the bringing of Agag is capped by the clause, "and/so Amalek have I devoted ["caused to be ḥrm"]". This clause may be taken simply as a parallel to the report in verse 8 ("and he devoted/utterly destroyed all the people [excluding Agag] with the edge of the sword") but may also be read as a more "summary" statement of his actions. Perhaps then we are to take it that Agag's fate is assumed in this summary clause?[7]

Thus the issue between Saul and Samuel on the matter of Agag may be viewed as similar to that on the matter of the spoil. Was it technically in defiance of the rules of ḥrm to bring the defeated king to Gilgal in order to slay him at the sanctuary? Should Agag have been lined up on the field of battle, or in his palace (or wherever), no doubt along with others who had survived the battle, and there executed? Saul apparently sees no problem in delaying the execution · and believes that he is acting in the spirit of the instruction; Samuel holds that the letter has been broken.

Several further small points need to be dealt with before we can discuss the implications of this interpretation of the scene.

(1) When assessing Saul's behaviour in this chapter commentators have sometimes cast doubt on his sincerity by another means. The following comment (Mauchline, 124) makes the point:

> The claim made by Saul to Samuel that he had fulfilled the commission was either a piece of bluster or bravado, or reveals a lack of awareness that he had done wrong which is well-nigh incredible. But any inclination to hold to the latter line for Saul's sake is surely made impossible when we read that Saul weakly attributes to the people the responsibility of reserving the best animals for sacrifice and so, implicitly, dissociating himself from the act and from responsibility for it.

This point rests on two grounds. First, it looks back to verse 9 where we are told that "Saul and the people spared Agag and the best of the sheep, etc."; thus, it is argued, the sparing of the spoil had been the act of both Saul and the people, in flat contradiction to Saul's claim in verse 21. The point looks well taken but it is far from being conclusive. A more sensitive reading of verse 9 might recognize a possible complexity of rhetorical style:[8] to say that "A and B spared C and D" may mean that "A spared C" and "B spared D" or, as we would say in English, "A and B spared C and D, respectively". When we look at Saul's explanation in verses 20f. we find him saying: "[1] I have brought Agag, the king of Amalek, and [2] I have devoted to destruction the Amalekites, [3] and the people have taken of the spoil, sheep and oxen, the best of the h̲rm-things to sacrifice to Yahweh your God in Gilgal". When we recognize the possibility of reading verse 9 as just indicated we have an appropriate correspondence; for the narrator tells us in verses 8 and 9 that: [1] Saul took Agag the king of the Amalekites alive, and [2] devoted to destruction all the people with the edge of the sword. And [1] Saul spared Agag, and [3] the people spared the best of the sheep, etc. Perhaps it is being over-subtle to say so, but it seems to me that the ambiguity in verse 9 is probably not accidental. Throughout this chapter the text teases us by setting the characters, especially Saul, in different lights, thereby contributing not only to the dramatic impact of the narrative but also to its capacity to stimulate the reader intellectually. To read the story, as is so often done, as though all were obvious is to underrate it.

The second ground on which rests the argument against Saul from verses 9f. is that, whether or not it was he or the people who spared the best of the spoil, it was he who was king and therefore he who was ultimately responsible. To divide responsibility or "pass the blame" is a sign of culpable weakness.[9] It is an accusation that is made explicit in Samuel's sarcastic response to Saul's talk of "the people":

"Though you are little in your own eyes, are you not the head of the tribes of Israel?"

Whatever justification there is in this mockery, it does not in fact (despite the insinuations of the commentators) have any bearing on the question of Saul's veracity. "Weak" he may (arguably) have been, but speaking the truth, nonetheless.

(2) A second point requiring clarification concerns Saul's confession of sin in verse 24. The RSV translates:

"I have sinned; for I have transgressed the commandment of the Lord and your words, because I feared the people and obeyed their voice".

Does this not suggest that he had known all along that he was in breach of the commandment, that he had acted against his better judgement through "fear" of the people? That interpretation is clearly possible. However, it is not the only way of understanding the passage, nor, I believe, the most probable. We have already seen that there is a strong case for viewing Saul as having acted in good faith, unaware that the distinction between ḥrm and zbḥ was of special religious importance. His explanation of this action had been of no avail. His second attempt to account for himself (verse 20f.) had been met with fierce rejection and an assertion, through the contrast of obedience and sacrifice, that Samuel (and so Yahweh) regarded the matter as of the utmost importance. Saul therefore has little choice but to acknowledge that as it now appears he has, after all, sinned, broken the strict terms of the command. Hertzberg (p. 126f.) notes that "Saul...is only convinced that he has done wrong during the course of his conversation with Samuel".[10] What he had been urged to do by the people and what he had clearly felt to be no serious deviation from his religious obligation has turned out to be a matter of major consequence. By speaking of the initiative of the people he is not weakly passing the blame but freely acknowledging his own error. The translation "fear" is misleading. The immediate context makes quite clear that it is not "terror" but "respect" or "honour" that is intended. Saul acknowledges that he has "transgressed the commandment of Yahweh". What a devout Israelite normally hopes to do is to "fear" (yr'), that is "respect" or "honour" Yahweh. The "because/for" clause (ky) is thus an appropriate rhetorical counterweight to the confession of sin; it draws a humbling implication, as if to say, "my action in going along with the people's wish has turned out to be tantamount to honouring them instead of Yahweh, obeying their voice instead of his commandments". Saul is not "wriggling" but expressing the deepest contrition possible in the circumstances.

Seen in the above light, then, the passage (verse 24) neither contradicts our earlier exegesis, that Saul acts throughout in good faith, nor adds any weight to an assessment of him as weakly attempting to shift the blame to others.

We are now in a position to pose again the question posed a little earlier. How culpable is Saul?

Saul's crime is either that he was ignorant of some technical implications of two sacral concepts (ḥrm and zbḥ) or, if he were aware of them, that he wrongly evaluated them

as unimportant (and therefore of no consequence in the fulfilling of the instructions). Samuel accuses him of disobedience. Clearly Saul considered himself obedient.
How culpable is Saul? Since he is depicted as acting in
good faith, then, on even the most rudimentary system of
morality, it is hard to see that he is being judged a moral
failure; his disobedience is neither wilful nor flagrant. Did
his unwitting disobedience have some dire moral consequences (apart from the consequences to himself!) or infringe
some major tenet of Israel's faith? How can we answer
other than "no"? - and few commentators have attempted to
show otherwise. Weiser (who accepts that Saul acts in good
faith) is at pains to show a theological difference between
the two concepts of hrm and zbh which he believes to be of
consequence for our assessment of Saul's action in condoning
the offering of hrm-things as sacrifice: hrm is man as God's
instrument (and thus living completely "in obedience") giving
back to God what is already decreed by God to be his; zbh is
offering something to God by man, as man, out of man's own
store; therefore to bring hrm-things for sacrifice is wrongly
to confuse the essential meaning of the two cultic acts.
This hypothesis may be right, we cannot be sure; even if it
were so what would it signify for Saul? A theological
"error", yes; an unwitting "sin", perhaps; but a sin of dev-
astating consequence, warranting God's rejection, surely not!
    Or is it then a matter of his having broken some
immutable law of the sacred, some powerful tabu? Hertzberg, who develops Weiser's thesis, seems at first to be
groping towards some such explanation (p. 127):

> Above all, however, Saul, by bringing the plunder
> undestroyed from the place of the "ban" [hrm], has
> thereby introduced it into the profane sphere of life,
> where it is exposed to the usual contamination.

But apart from the fact that the plunder was being
introduced into a sanctuary, hardly a "profane sphere of
life", this kind of suggestion still runs into the difficulty
that if it were really a matter of such import is it not
strange that it was unknown to any but Samuel? The irony
is that Hertzberg discusses the problem in the context of
the following remark (p. 127):

> Behind this conversation [between Saul and Samuel]

54

lies the question whether the "ban" and sacrifice are equivalent, as Saul first assumes. The discussion of this is particularly important, because it recalls the criticism of sacrificial worship in classical prophecy.

However, if Weiser and Hertzberg are right that there is an important difference at stake, then Samuel stands not for the (classical) prophetic vein of religion over against the priestly or sacrificial, but the other way round, for he is seen to be championing the necessity for the strictest formal observance of sacred rites.

This point is important for it makes it more difficult to sustain an argument that in chapter 13, ambiguous instruction notwithstanding, Saul's choice of interpretation indicates lack of a proper faith, an absolute dependence on the prophet ("wait until I come"), whereas Saul places weight on the necessity for cultic observances in the critical circumstances. Chapter 15 makes doubly clear that the judgement against Saul is not a matter of his rejecting prophetic religion, since the (formal) basis of condemation is a technical nicety of cultic religion. Significantly the narrative offers a picture of conflict between prophetic and cultic religion and to this extent those commentators who see this conflict as the key to the rejection (the story champions the prophetic word against cultic practice) are not entirely off the mark. But a thorough reading cannot ignore the complication woven into the account of the rejection, namely that in both chapter 13 and chapter 15 the judgment against Saul hinges on a matter of cultic propriety.[11] In other words the story cannot just be paraphrased in terms of conventional doctrine (inner disposition/obedience to the word versus outward form/concern for cultic religion). It is too complex for that.

To return to the question of hrm and zbh, then, I conclude that such theorizing as Weiser and Hertzberg attempt is unnecessary. Nor are there sufficient clues in the text to sustain it. The precise meaning of these terms remains obscure and it is difficult not to agree with those remarks of Soggin's (p. 195) which began this analysis:

To the modern reader Saul might hardly seem to be a "sinner", and we might doubt whether his "sin" made much impression on the reader or hearer of that time.

Thus, on the interpretation I have just sketched, it becomes otiose to seek an underlying reason for Saul's failure - such as greed, irreligion, desire for public "face", lack of faith, emotional insecurity, lack of self-esteem, "wilfulness", or mental instability, to mention but a few that have found advocates - for here in chapter 15, as in chapter 13, there is essentially no failure on Saul's part to be accounted for, no failure, that is to say, for which he can be held seriously culpable.[12]

We noted that the sparing of Agag was the point in Saul's account of himself that raised the biggest question mark. We also saw that there was reason to interpret this action too as taken in good faith. But what is really important for our understanding of the story is that Samuel does not bother to question him on this one point where Saul's explanation seems most potentially vulnerable. Rather Samuel chooses to ignore the explanation altogether and to respond to the king's protestations merely with fine rhetoric (verse 22f.). Again (as in chapter 13), therefore, the real point of the scene can only be that in some way Saul is already doomed and that any detailed justification for his condemnation is essentially irrelevant. As with the command to wait at Gilgal, the command to destroy Amalek may be interpreted in such a way that Saul be deemed to have disobeyed it. The privilege of interpretation belongs, of course, to God, and God, allowing no explanation on Saul's part, chooses to interpret as he does. Even when, by the end of Saul's altercation with Samuel, it appears that he is in effect being convicted on a technicality, that fact appears to be of no consequence. A technicality seems to be all that is required.

The story thus forces us to re-examine, not Saul's conduct and motives, but those of Samuel and Yahweh. Why do they hold such a rigid pose? Why is Saul's penitence disregarded? Why is Saul rejected? We are back at the fundamental question.

Part Two
THE STORY

...in Aeschylean phrase...
Hardy, <u>Tess of the d'Urbervilles</u>

Chapter Four
THE STORY: 1 SAMUEL 8-15

Prologue (1 Samuel 8)

That Yahweh is to be a significant factor in the story is made clear at the outset, in what we might call the "prologue" (chapter 8), and in the story of Saul's anointing as king which follows. Likewise Samuel's key standing as confidant and agent of Yahweh is brought home from the beginning. To call chapter 8 a "prologue" is not to suggest that it is a mere appendage; on the contrary, in it lie the seeds of the main story.

The established system of leadership, by "judge" (špṭ) has failed. Samuel has resigned his judgeship in favour of his sons but they have turned out to be corrupt. In desperation, the elders of Israel seek a remedy in a change of system - why not have a "king" to "govern" (špṭ) and lead in battle (verses 5 and 20) like everybody else?[1] Why a king should be any better than a judge is of no interest to our narrator. More significant is the response of Samuel and Yahweh. Samuel is "displeased" ("and the thing was evil in the sight of Samuel"). But why? He himself has recognized his own incapacity in the matter (by abdicating on account of his old age) and it is his own sons who are the immediate cause of the problem. Yahweh's reassurance - "they have not rejected you [as you suppose]" - suggests that Samuel's displeasure is on account of his own self-regard. Yahweh's response is also that of displeasure. He alone is "king" of Israel and to him the people's desire for an earthly king is a denigration of his own kingship: he likens the action to the disloyalty of the people in former times "forsaking me and serving other gods". Both characters, therefore, might be regarded as having taken the people's request as a personal affront.

59

Yahweh's reaction contains a key term: the people, he says, have "rejected" (m's) him. When Samuel in chapter 10 gathers the people at Mizpah to choose a king, he delivers Yahweh's word to them, reiterating his understanding of the people's request for a king as a "rejection" of his own kingship (10:19):

> You have this day rejected (m's) your God, who saves you from all your calamities and your distresses; and you have said, "No! but set a king over us".

The term m's next occurs again in our story in the context of Yahweh's rejection of Saul (15:23):[2]

> Because you have rejected (m's) the word of Yahweh he has also rejected (m's) you from being king.

The only other occurrence of the term is in 16:7, with Yahweh's word to Samuel that he is not to look on the appearance or height of Eliab because he has "rejected" him. The scene of course follows hard on the "rejection" of Saul, and is indeed the implementation of that rejection: with the description of Eliab we are doubly reminded of Saul (cf. 9:2 and 10:23). The use of the motif of rejection thus formally links Saul's fate with Yahweh's understanding of his own treatment at the hands of the people. We shall return to this connection further in the final chapter (Seven).

Despite his strong sense of grievance, Yahweh does not hesitate. His first words to Samuel are (astonishingly, for one so aggrieved): "Obey ("hearken to the voice of" - šm' bqwl) the people in all that they say to you" (8:7). His repetition of this instruction, before adding that Samuel should first warn the people of the perils of earthly kingship, suggests that, for Yahweh, the warning by Samuel is no more than a formality. Yahweh expects the people to "refuse to obey (šm' bqwl)" Samuel and insist on having an earthly king; the warning merely serves to underline their wilfulness in "rejecting" their true king.

Sure enough, Samuel's words fall on deaf ears. Nor (looking at it from the people's point of view) is this surprising considering that he has offered no constructive counter-proposal to meet the people's need. Yahweh's response is reiterated a third time with a curt, "Obey (šm' bqwl) them and make them a king".

60

The Story: 1 Samuel 8-15

What is the spirit of this compromise? Is it open-hearted generosity? Simple resignation? Or, bearing in mind the un-wavering determination of this response, is it a concession which conceals a deep-seated conviction that the wrongness of the people's request will inevitably become manifest, must become manifest, as if to say, "Hearken to their voice, and make them a king - and let us see what we shall see!". Is, then, the instruction to "obey the people" an ironical one? That interpretation presses itself upon one. There is little gracious acquiescence here; and Samuel's instruction to the people is equally curt.

Thus chapter 8 presents us with two figures whose potential for influencing future events is clearly great. They may also be two figures nursing a grievance. We have been warned against expecting the forthcoming experiment in kingship to be an unmitigated success.

Saul's rise (1 Samuel 9-12)

The story of Saul's anointing begins brightly enough. He is fine lad who prosecutes his errand, looking for his father's asses, with vigour and a nice concern for his parent (9:5). Fate rapidly works its way into the pattern of events: the young man would have turned back but for his servant's chance find of money to provide a gift to the seer; fortuitously, also, Saul discovers Samuel at just the moment when he is able to join the ritual feast. The reader soon knows that Saul's expedition is pre-ordained by Yahweh (verse 16); Saul learns the same thing through Samuel's demonstration that he was expecting him (verses 23f.). Furthermore there is now a comforting hint of benevolent motivation behind Yahweh's involvement in the events - he has heard the cry of his people, we are told, and it is to be Saul who will deliver them from their enemies, the Philistines (verse 16).

The story of the unlikely hero (cf. verse 21) rapidly moves (through a series of oblique disclosures) to the anointing an astonishing end to the search for Kish's asses - and to the giving of further signs as proof of the "reality" of Saul's designation as potential king ("chief", "prince" - nāgîd). The third, and climactic, sign is the seizure of Saul by the spirit of prophecy. Saul, at least momentarily, is given the status of prophet (like Samuel) and is thereby apparently marked out as Yahweh's servant.

A few elements of interest invite comment. The anointing takes place in the context of a sacrifice/feast; a sacrifice is also the context of David's anointing, later, when Saul has been rejected, though ironically the main reason for the sacrifice on that occasion seems to be in order to provide a cover story for the visit to Jesse, in order to deceive Saul! The sacrifice does not only provide resonances for that later anointing episode; it is also linked to the first scene of rejection (chapter 13). When we read there of Saul's predicament in waiting for Samuel to come to the sacrifice we are prompted to remember Saul's first introduction to Samuel (9:11-3):

> As they went up the hill to the city they met young maidens coming out to draw water, and said to them, "Is the seer here?". They answered, "He is; behold he is just ahead of you. Make haste (mhr); he has come just now (hyywm) to the city, because the people have a sacrifice today (hyywm) on the high place. As soon as you enter the city you will find him, before he goes up to the high place to eat; for the people will not eat till he comes, since he must bless the sacrifice; afterwards those eat who are invited. Now go up, for you will meet him immediately (hyywm)".

Here (chapter 9) it is all urgency, for the prophet is "ahead of" Saul and Saul must make haste to catch up before he officiates at the sacrifice; there (chapter 13) it is all urgency, but the urgency is for the sacrifice to take place and it is the prophet who lags behind. Saul's haste in the one scene leads to success, in the other to disaster. In chapter 13 he decides to wait no longer for the prophet. The remark in chapter 9 comes back to us: "for the people will not eat till he comes, since he must bless the sacrifice".

The crucial instruction regarding Gilgal comes as the episode draws near to an end (10:7f.). It sits amongst the other instructions of the prophet, a seemingly innocuous item, one amongst a number; and to lend to the feeling of the smooth flow of fortune here, the other items are quickly met and fulfilled without apparent disharmony.

One final point: the spirit of God comes mightily upon Saul and he "prophecies"/"raves" (wayyitnabbē') in the midst of a band of prophets. We are told (verses 11f.) that the people said to one another, "What has come over the son of Kish? Is Saul also among the prophets?" And a man of the place answered, "And who is their father?" Therefore it became a proverb, "Is Saul also among the prophets?".

The precise significance of this "proverb" has long been debated by commentators.[3] I do not wish to enter the debate; rather I would merely observe that at issue in context is whether the saying indicates a positive or negative attitude towards Saul. This question, in turn, is tied up with that of what attitude towards the "prophesying" prophetic band is implied here. In the present context it would seem that Saul's "prophesying" is being presented as a positive sign - that, as I have described it above, he is given the status of prophet (like Samuel) and thereby marked out as Yahweh's servant. Yet as we shall see, later in the story (19:23f. and cf. 18:10), compulsion to prophesy can be a sign of Saul's rejection. McKane is on the right lines, I think, when he comments (p. 124) on 19:23f.:

> Saul is still possessed by spiritual forces, but this possession is now the evidence of his rejection ....Ecstasy once made him free and able to do Yahweh's will, but now it evidences his derangement and slavery.

"Prophesying" can be "raving". It is, therefore, an ambiguous gift. Perhaps, therefore, it is no accident that the stance of the proverb is so elusive. In itself the proverb expresses surprise, perhaps even incongruity. It is its context that determines whether it is disparaging or not; but even if here in chapter 10 it may be taken positively, its ambiguity lends yet another hint of a dark tone to Saul's success.

A lull in the story follows (10:14-6). The private designation of Saul as "prince" is then succeeded, in verses 17-27, by public designation as king, again the divine choice being indicated by "chance" (here the lot). Yet once more there is present a strong negative undertone. Samuel introduces the proceedings with nothing other than a restatement of Yahweh's complaint against the people for their desire to have a king. Moreover, at the end there is a further complication with the expression of scepticism by some of the Israelites: "'How can this man serve us?' And they despised him, and brought him no present" (10:27).

The third phase in Saul's way to the throne is the deliverance of Jabesh-Gilead. As the divine spirit had seized him and caused him to prophesy at the time of his anointing, so now it emboldens him to make a challenge to all Israel to come to the help of the besieged city. The aftermath shows us a magnanimous Saul who spares the life of those who had earlier opposed him (11:12f.; cf. David's similar response in 2 Samuel 16:5-12 and 19:18-23) and who ascribes to Yahweh the victory. With this test behind him Saul's kingship is "renewed" (confirmed?) "before Yahweh in Gilgal", with great rejoicing by all the people. As for Samuel's instruction of 10:8, we are left uncertain as to whether or not it has been fulfilled in this event.

Chapter 12 brings us back to the theme of Samuel and Yahweh and the principle of kingship. If Saul and the men of Israel are rejoicing greatly, Samuel is not. The first part of his speech appears defensive, self-protective: the old has made way for the new - is there any complaint outstanding against the old? Again we are given a hint of Samuel's sense of personal rejection. Old age and his sons he mentions as though they were incidental to the whole matter. In the light of chapter 8 they clearly are not. Yet the people without further ado bear witness loyally to Samuel's personal integrity - and thereby appear to put themselves in the wrong. If they have nothing against Samuel why then should they have demanded a king? The prophet now moves easily into a broader attack. He attacks them for their history of disloyalty to Yahweh. This history is apparently one of Yahweh's deliverance of his people out of, and into, oppression. The key to the people's fortune is their undivided loyalty to God. Since Yahweh alone is king of Israel, the demand for another king is disloyalty.

So far the speech has simply recapitulated, or amplified, the complaint of chapter 8. Not that this recapitulation is insignificant. On the contrary it shows us that the affront is still keenly felt. But we know, and the people know, that Yahweh has made a compromise and has, in fact, chosen a king. So now the terms of the compromise are spelt out a little more clearly: the king must recognize his subordination to the king of kings - to hearken to the voice of Yahweh (and by implication, his prophet) and obey his commandment is absolutely essential if Yahweh is not to turn against both king and people. And to demonstrate finally that his word is indeed God's word, and that the power he represents is a power to be reckoned with, Samuel invokes the ruin of the harvest.[4]

At no point in the the scene does anyone remonstrate with Samuel, even though it is apparent that no one is particularly convinced that the move to kingship was a wrong one: in the face of the thunder and rain the people confess a sin and ask that they may not die, but nowhere in the scene do we find anyone suggesting that the decision for kingship be revoked. The people recognize the power that confronts them and do what is expected of them. For most people, in the face of divine anger, that is wisdom. It is significant that it is only Saul, in the whole story, who remonstrates directly with Yahweh or his prophet (chapter 15) and even then his self-assertion is short-lived (and like the people here he confesses his "sin").

The scene thus ends with Samuel totally in control. He it is who will pray for the people, despite their present lapse, and he it is who will instruct them in what is right. "But if you do wickedly, you shall be swept away, both you and your king" (12:25).

So the precariousness of Saul's position is made doubly clear as the first act of his story is rounded off. Not only is he a secondary figure in Yahweh's scheme of things, but he walks a tightrope. He is caught in the midst of a situation of tension which is not of his own making and over which he has but limited control. To the reader it is now growing obvious that there is likely to be little room for error in Saul's conduct as king, and if fault is to be found in him it is likely to be in the matter of "obedience". Saul is vassal to an overlord who seems fundamentally hostile and Saul is potentially vulnerable as an object-lesson by Yahweh to a people who are less than totally committed to their God.

Saul the king: the Philistines (1 Samuel 13-14)

The next main section of the story opens with Saul engaged in his first major exercise of kingship - a campaign against the Philistines. Right at the beginning we get a further strong hint that success is not going to come Saul's way readily: it is Jonathan who defeats the Philistines at

Geba, a point which is only accentuated by the subsequent rumour, that Saul had defeated them (13:4f.). In the event the Philistine army that confronts Saul at Michmash (13:5) is a massive one. Not unnaturally the people begin to desert or at least fail to rally to the king. Saul waits at Gilgal, disaster staring him in the face. He waits for <u>Samuel</u> (verse 8). Suddenly, for the reader, the tension is doubled. The Philistine threat is only one aspect of the potential disaster; with verse 8 we know that here at last is the situation corresponding to the command of 10:8, and we now know (in the light of chapter 12) that it is a situation fraught with risk for Saul.

He waited for seven days, the time appointed by Samuel; but Samuel did not come to Gilgal, and the people were scattering from him.

As his later explanation makes clear (verses 11f.), Saul feels that it is imperative that the proper religious rite be performed, both to boost morale and to ensure that the Israelites are properly prepared (according to religious law) for a battle that could ensue at any time. As earlier in the matter of Jabesh-Gilead he is decisive. He acts as he thinks his responsibilities as king demand and decides to wait for the tardy prophet no longer. He offers the sacrifice himself. But (verse 10),

as soon as he had finished offering the burnt-offering, behold, Samuel came.

This sentence as much as any other encapsulates the predicament of Saul. He appears here starkly as the plaything of fate. Can this extraordinary timing of Samuel's arrrival be merely accidental, we wonder? The urgency with which Saul moves into the attack is instructive,too. Saul's explanation of his action is brushed aside without even cursory consideration: Saul, declaims the prophet, has not obeyed God's command and stands condemned. Nor is the king given any opportunity to beg mercy of God. It is as though that condemnation, and the accompanying judgement, was the primary object of Samuel's visit. At the very least we might say that Samuel (which must mean God) has seized this opportunity with both hands.
The question that immediately arises at this point is the ·

one we have already examined (above, chapter two): On
what grounds has Saul been condemned? - for nowhere are
they precisely stated. As we saw, the condemnation is most
readily seen as deriving from the instruction of 10:8; and it
is unlikely that the propriety of the sacrifice being offered
by other than a prophet or priest is really at issue. The
answer to the question lies rather in the ambiguity of the
instruction: while it may seem that Saul has fulfilled the
conditions of the command, in that he has waited the required seven days, the instruction also speaks of him being
required to wait "until I come to you". It is the ambiguity
that becomes the trap.
     So Saul is caught.
     It is important to note that the judgement also is
ambiguous: at the least it means that Saul will not establish
a dynasty; at the most it could be taken to mean that his
kingship will come to an immediate end - for a successor is
already chosen. Thus Saul acts henceforth knowing that
unless he can manage to defy this destiny, he has himself no
certain future as a king, while Jonathan his son has no
future at all. (It is all the more ironical, then, that it is
Jonathan who achieves most of what military success comes
Israel's way in the Philistine campaign.) For Saul there
remains only the dignity of pressing on with the task in hand.
     Jonathan's sortie against the Philistines in chapter 14 not
only develops the motif at the beginning of chapter 13 - it is
Jonathan, not Saul, who exhibits military prowess - it also
illustrates that, despite the condemnation of Saul, Yahweh
is still on the side of Israel. We may be prompted to recall
that amongst the more ominous tones of the beginning of
the story, there was also that expression of goodwill in 9:16,

> He [Saul] shall save my people from the hand of the
> Philistines; for I have seen the affliction of my people
> because their cry has come to me".

Jonathan puts his trust in Yahweh ("it may be that Yahweh
will work for us", 14:6), wreaks astonishing havoc, and has
his exploit marked at the end by a panic and earthquake that
can only come from God. The battle grows and not even
Saul's involvement seems able to contain the extent of his
victory (14:16-23).
     At this point, however, another complication for Saul

arises. No sooner has the story moved to a peak ("so Yahweh delivered Israel that day", verse 23) than the narrator undercuts the mood of triumph and slows down the pace (14:23f.):

> And the battle passed beyond Beth-aven. And the men of Israel were distressed that day, for Saul had laid an oath on the people.

The battle starts quite independently of Saul, through Jonathan's foray, which at first no one else knows about, least of all Saul. The king's pious vow, imposing a fast on the army as a token of devotion to Yahweh, then ensnares an unsuspecting Jonathan who, precisely because of his succesful, _divinely aided,_ initiation of the battle, knows nothing of it. It would seem that Saul is to be allowed a victory only at a cost - and the cost is to be exacted, ironically, through the agent of victory. The king triggers the complication by his own action, but only through the mechanism of the "chance" absence of Jonathan and the "fortuitous" abundance of honey in the forest into which the pursuit happens to move.

Jonathan's response, on being informed of his infringement, is for the first time openly critical of his father.[5] He takes a pragmatic view: the honey has revived him ("see how my eyes have become bright", 14:29) and food would have sustained the army in a more vigorous mopping-up of the enemy. The response thus has the function of pointing up the _piety_ of the king's action.

In fact the problem for Saul grows, for in desperation the people fall upon (reading y't) the live-stock of their enemies and eat it in a way that breaks the ritual law (14:31f.), so that Saul is forced to withdraw his attention from the battle and provide a make-shift arrangement in order to ensure proper cultic observance (14:34f.). The oath, therefore, however well-intentioned, is shown to have proved disastrous in practice. It is as though God has thrown it back in Saul's face.

Worse is to come, That evening, dutifully consulting the priestly oracle before furthering the attack on the Philistines, Saul learns of Yahweh's displeasure, and when an elimination is made by lot (an ironic reminder of Saul's designation as king)[6] it becomes apparent to the king that

The Story: 1 Samuel 8-15

Jonathan is the offender. At this point the narrator presents us with another great irony, for Saul behaves now towards Jonathan, his own son, in just the same unbending way as Samuel had earlier behaved towards him, Saul, in the matter of his "breaking" Samuel's instruction to wait for him at Gilgal. No allowance is made for the circumstances of Jonathan's sin. The undeniable fact of it is enough. Saul simply condemns him to death. In Saul's case, of course, there is a positive as well as a negative side to his response - negative, in that he exhibits an inappropriate rigidity of attitude; positive, in that he has done what he has done with the interests of his people at heart and at the sacrifice of his own (family) interest (as is the case with Jonathan who with simple dignity offers to die). He is doubly trapped, since (with unconscious irony) he has already sworn (verse 39) that if it be he or his son who is culpable then he or his son should die.

So the story switches direction dramatically, moving from success to disaster; and the pious oath, which at first seems the cause of only minor complication, issues finally in a terrible dilemma for the king.

Resolution comes through the people (verse 45). They too adopt the pragmatic view and refuse to allow the death of the one person who had most distinguished himself ("wrought with God") that day. Saul's dilemma is resolved, but at the cost of another oath broken (that of 14:39) and with a significant abdication of authority. In the end it is the people who rule, not Saul the king. Yet that is perhaps as it should be; for it is the ordinary, humane, commonsense view that prevails. Indeed there has been a curious shift in Saul's role in this episode. It is as though, in reaction to the circumstances of his condemnation at Gilgal, he has been playing the role of a Samuel, giving token of his acceptance of God's absolute priority over all merely human considerations (as in the oath) and demanding strict and uncompromising compliance with the divine scheme of things (as in his preparedness to execute Jonathan). It is Jonathan and the people who play the role that Saul had played at Gilgal. In a sense, therefore, in accepting the people's refusal to allow the (humanly speaking) absurd to happen, Saul becomes himself again.

One further consideration arising from this episode of

69

the oath: given the swearing of the oath as an initiating cause in the sequence of trouble, have we an indication that perhaps Saul's problem is to be sought within himself? Is he · prone to be rash? And may we then look back to his sacrifice at Gilgal and wonder if there also he was hastily decisive, unduly pressured by events? Should he have exercised a little more patience? Such an interpretation is not easily dismissed. On the other hand, our observation in the preceding paragraph concerning the circumstances of the oath-swearing, and the remembrance of that so-delicately-timed delay by Samuel at Gilgal is sufficient to bring back into focus that other perspective, of Saul as a victim, while the series of "accidents" vital to the cause-and-effect chain in the oath story reinforces a judgement that, whatever Saul's failings, he has much to contend with that lies beyond his control.

The immediate outcome of all this trouble is that no further action is taken in the battle against the Philistines. Both sides withdraw. The section ends (14:47-52) with a brief recital of Saul's campaigns against enemies on all sides, with some measure of success; and perhaps in verses 47f. we are indeed to see the fulfilment of Yahweh's promise in 9:16 that Saul would save the people from the hand of the Philistines. If so, the last verse of the chapter (14:52: "there was hard fighting against the Philistines all the days of Saul") may warn us that, strictly speaking, the promise leaves open the possibility of a complete reversal of fortune as well.[7]

Saul the king: the Amalekites (1 Samuel 15)

Saul's second major experience in the exercise of kingship is his campaign against the Amalekites. The episode begins with instructions from Samuel, so that we are immediately aware that Saul is in another "obedience" situation. Nothing is said of the earlier judgement against the king. Samuel simply states his authority, implicitly reminding the king of his vassal status, and issues his command to attack and destroy Amalek.

We have already looked closely at this chapter and the way it narrates the story of Saul's "disobedience" over the matter of the spoil, swinging our sympathy now away from, now back to, the king. As was the case with chapter 13, we

70

The Story: 1 Samuel 8-15

saw that here too there is every reason to take it that Saul
acts in good faith. And again, Samuel's refusal to accord
Saul's explanation even the most cursory consideration
(exemplified most markedly in his disdaining to ask about
Agag) leads us, as in chapter 13, to conclude that judgement
wil be made against Saul for "disobedience" irrespective of
any good faith in the motivation of his action. The scene,
like that in chapter 13, discloses to the reader that Saul
when "tested" is bound to fail. That is his fate.

Within the story itself, the king too knows what his response must be to the prophet's condemnation. He realizes
that he is trapped once again and that he can do nothing
other than submit. He confesses that after all he has sinned
(recognizing that he cannot contest Yahweh's - or his prophet's - definition of "sin"). Whether there is a mischievous
distinction intended in his reference to "Yahweh's commandment and your words" we cannot be sure. At any rate he
asks pardon and requests permission to be allowed continued
access to the worship of God. The reader knows now,
however, that this is useless.

Samuel rejects Saul as king, on Yahweh's behalf, and
turns the robe-tearing to his purpose of judgement: the kingdom is torn from Saul "this day" and given to a neighbour
who is "better" than he. Thus the judgement of chapter 13
is confirmed. But while the phrase "this day" seems to lend
it an immediacy and the term "neighbour" a specificity it
did not previously have, the judgement still retains that
openness that characterized the first rejection. All Saul can
truly know is that he finds no favour with God; the moment
of his removal from the throne is still not disclosed to him.
So Samuel rejects him, on Yahweh's behalf. Nor, he adds,
will Yahweh "repent" of his action.

The rest of the scene is one of pathos. Saul asks for at
least a token show of honour before his people, and Samuel,
with little to lose - after all, he knows now that Saul is
irretrievably doomed and that Yahweh, in due course, will
be vindicated - accommodates him. So, ironically, the scene
ends with the "disobedient" Saul worshipping Yahweh.

For his part Samuel takes the completion of the ḥrm (or
so it seems) into his own hands and deals with Agag. His
sentiment is human - "As your sword has made women
childless, so shall your mother be childless among women"

(15:33) - but his action lacks humanity. But to seek humanity in Samuel is to mistake his role. He is like Teiresias in Sophocles' King Oedipus. He is the mouthpiece and agent of forces beyond him. He has no choice but to give effect to the intractable demands of divine decree, the dictates of fate:[8]

> So Samuel hewed Agag in pieces before Yahweh in Gilgal.

"Before Yahweh in Gilgal" is like a refrain in this story, for before Yahweh in Gilgal take place the key events in these first formative episodes. The phrase thus speaks to us of Saul as well as of Yahweh and his prophet.

The scene ends with the short summary sentence:

> So Yahweh repented that he had made Saul king over Israel.

It is as if to say that the episode has been about not only Saul's "sin" but even more, perhaps, Yahweh's "repentance". The sentence picks up the theme of verse 11, Yahweh's word to Samuel:

> "I repent that I have made Saul king; for he has turned back from following me, and has not performed my commandments".

It also forces our attention again to the remarkable discrepancy between these lines and Samuel's assertion in verse 29 of Yahweh's divine immutability.

As a question to a humbled Saul, Samuel's words in 28f. work well: Saul has embarked on a course of action and now wishes to "repent"; Yahweh too has now embarked on a course of action - the designation of another king in Saul's place - but he, being no mere man (like Saul), will not "repent" (which term in the context clearly has connotations of change of heart/attitude). To the omniscient reader (who has read verse 11 and will read verse 34), however, the rhetoric gives rise to serious misgivings. Does God "repent" or not? What does Samuel really believe (given verse 11)? Is it possible that the prophet's confidant-sounding assertion that God will not repent may mask a deep unease on the subject (that is to say, is he over-compensating)? That may be too subtle a conclusion. But the point I wish to make is that the way the text focusses on this matter of Yahweh's "repentance" is to raise questions about it.

On the one hand, the word of Yahweh to Samuel in verse 11 sounds straightforward enough. Because Saul has broken his commandments (as Yahweh sees it) Yahweh has repented of giving him the kingship; that is, he will now take the kingship away. On the other hand, indicators in the story so far (including chapter 15) have suggested that the basis of the judgement against Saul, the "repentance" of Yahweh, is more complex than this simple explanation ("because") suggests; Yahweh's dealings with Saul are, shall we say, less · than impartial. Our feeling, therefore, is likely to be that there is more to Yahweh's "repentance" than verse 11 discloses. Such a feeling can only be reinforced when verses 11, 29 and 35 (taken in concert) themselves set a question mark against the nature of God's "repentance" and invite us to look a little further. Accordingly we shall come back to this question, in the Chapter Seven.

Chapter 15 is obviously a pivotal scene in the story. By the end of the chapter Saul's rejection as king by Yahweh is beyond all further doubt. The actual process of rejection, however, has set up some interesting contrasts. Chapter 8 began the story with a question about "judging" (šp̱ṯ) which · led to the making of a king. From the final appointment of Saul in chapter 11, the major episodes (chapters 12-15) have all centred around important judgements. In chapter 12 Samuel upbraids the people for their sin against Yahweh (and himself) in asking for a king, passes judgement on them and calls upon Yahweh to ruin their wheat harvest with a storm. The people's response is to ask that Samuel should pray for them to Yahweh, owning that their request for a king was a sin. Samuel's response is one of reassurance: "Fear not!...For Yahweh will not cast away his people".

The judgement against Saul in chapter 13 is peremptory - there is no pause to consider the king's response - but that in chapter 15 offers a nice parallel to the judgement in chapter 12. Saul in the position of penitent receives, of course, strikingly different treatment from Samuel's treatment of the people: to his acknowledgment of sin and his request for Samuel to return with him in order that he might worship Yahweh, the prophet refuses outright to have anything more to do with him, though to further entreaties he does accommodate the wish to worship Yahweh. But there is no pardon as there is for the people in chapter 12.

As we have observed, Saul's condemnation of Jonathan echoes Samuel's unbending mode of "judging". Again the contrast with the Samuel scenes is striking, for a satisfactory resolution is reached only by the timely and sensible intervention of the people who demand, in effect, that the religious laws be bent to accommodate the realities of the situation. It is tempting to conclude that it is neither Saul the "king" nor Samuel the "judge", but the people who turn out to know best what "judging" is about!

Chapter 14 is, of course, not the only place where Saul listens to the people. In chapter 15 he owns to having "obeyed the people" (verse 24) and we have already seen that this admission is often marked against Saul as a sign of weakness, a sign of his little deserving to be a king. There is a rather charming irony in the charge, for it is precisely the autocratic king who far from obeying the people will oppress them with his every whim, whom Samuel urges against the people in chapter 8 as a reason for not having a king at all! The observation of "weakness" on Saul's part, therefore, merely underscores the fact that whatever Saul is being condemned for, it is nothing to do with Samuel's list of royal horrors. Whether his "listening to the voice of the people" is a weakness or strength lies, I believe, in the eye of the reader.

Chapter 15 is about a judgement; it is also about "obedience". The phrase "listen to the voice of Yahweh" ("obey"- šmʿ bqwl) punctuates the speeches and reminds us of chapter 8 where its use was nearly as frequent.[9] We observed a probable undertone of irony in Yahweh's instruction to Samuel to "obey (šmʿ bqwl) the people". That irony is confirmed now in chapter 15 where we find Saul being condemned for doing precisely what Samuel had been ordered to do:

"I have sinned...for I honoured [feared?] the people and obeyed their voice".

In the divine sphere of operation "obeying the people" is implicitly opposed to "obeying the god" and can only produce negative results. It is appropriate that Saul, whose appointment as king came from "obeying the people" should meet with rejection through "obeying the people".

The Story: 1 Samuel 8-15

So Saul's formal rejection is complete. The remainder of the story is a matter of either how the rejection will be implemented in practice, or whether Saul can cheat his fate. On previous indications the reader may well doubt the likelihood of the latter alternative; but one of the more fascinating aspects of the story itself is that Saul, despite foreknowledge of his fate as decreed by God, strives almost to the last to maintain his hold on the kingship. To this extent he retains a spark of independence as a character and his role is not simply a reflection of Yahweh's divine intentions. Yet paradoxically the more he struggles against his fate - which from now on is increasingly embodied in the figure of David - the more he himself becomes fate's agent. In this regard, as in others, the reader who wishes to set our story in a wider literary context will find some interesting parallels between this story and that, say, of Sophocles' King Oedipus or Shakespeare's Macbeth.

Chapter Five
THE STORY: 1 SAMUEL 16-23

Saul and his rival:
David at court (I Samuel 16-19:17)

The new phase in the story introduces David and explores his relationship with Saul at court. From the outset it is made clear to the reader that David is to be Saul's successor, but Saul is left to divine that for himself. The anointing of David is carried out by subterfuge involving, ironically, the pretence that the real purpose of Samuel's excursion is to offer a sacrifice.[1] Two other points may be noted at the very beginning of this section of the story. Samuel claims that were Saul to hear of his mission he (Saul) would kill him. Is this a touch of paranoia on Samuel's part, or is it an intimation of a violent strain in Saul that will begin to mark his life from now on? (Should we find, then, a kernel of this characteristic back in chapter 11, in the violence of that message to the men of Israel to come to the rescue of Jabesh-Gilead?) Furthermore, the tense atmosphere of suspicion and potential violence is not confined to relations between Yahweh/Samuel and Saul. The elders of Bethlehem meet Samuel with fear and barely disguised hostility (16:4f.). To ordinary people, as to kings, Samuel can be a dangerous man.[2]

The choice and anointing of David takes place (16:6-13). Like Saul, David is a "least likely hero", the youngest of the brothers. Like Saul, too, he is a handsome youth. One wonders whether it is with conscious or unconscious irony that the narrator, having had Yahweh deliver his fine sentiments in verse 7 ("Do not look on his [Eliab's] appearance....Man looks on the outward appearance but Yahweh looks on the

heart"), introduces David with no other recommendation
than that David "was ruddy, and had beautiful eyes, and was
handsome". Presumably, however, the outward appearance
is fortuitous (or perhaps a concession to man's weakness!).
We have already been told that Yahweh's choice was of "a
man after his own heart" (13:14); so Samuel anoints the
young man. If, looking back to Saul's anointing, we wait for
God's command to David, we wait in vain. Where Saul's kingship had been immediately hedged around with provisions,
David's is left open. No trap is set for the new king.
Clearly David's fate has been marked out very differently
from Saul's.

As earlier had been the experience of Saul, the spirit of
Yahweh comes mightily on David. Yahweh is with him. For
Saul, on the other hand, the experience is reversed (16:14):

Now the spirit of Yahweh departed from Saul, and an
evil spirit from Yahweh tormented him.

Here for the first time explicitly we have Welch's "dark
powers" (cf. the discussion in Chapter One, above). Again,
therefore, we are confronted with the theme of Saul the
victim, and this theme competes for our sympathy during
our growing alienation from Saul as he becomes ever more
moody, jealous and violent.

There is no flabbiness in the narrative at this point. The
introduction of the spirit tormenting Saul leads directly to
David's involvement in Saul's life. By the cruellest of fate's
tricks no sooner is David anointed and Saul unwell (poisoned
by Yahweh, one might say) than his own servants are
recommending David as the cure for his sickness. The eco-
nomy of plot is superb and the irony of the situation that is
created is quite overwhelming. "Behold", says Saul's servant
(16:18), "I have seen a son of Jesse the Bethlehemite, who is
skilful in playing, a man of valour, a man of war, prudent in
speech, and a man of good presence"; and, as though this
were not enough, he adds, "and Yahweh is with him" - as if
to underline the fact that Yahweh is not with Saul![3] In
many respects 16:14-23 is the rest of the story in micro-
cosm. With an introductory nudge by fate, Saul delivers
himself into the hands of David. The king provides the youth
with the opportunity to gain the status of an alternative
king, and Saul becomes totally dependent on David's

goodwill for his survival. Thus, right at the beginning of his career, David is shown to have the upper hand - as befits God's new servant.

Just as Saul's rise to prominence had been pictured in several stages, so now with David. Secretly anointed, then brought to court in a role ancillary to the king, he is finally put to public test. The plot is flawed at the end of chapter 16 - we need some mention of his being sent home from court and perhaps of his appearance, as he matures, being greatly altered so as not to be recognizable on his re-appearance before Saul and his general.[4] Be that as it may, the movement of the story in chapter 17 can carry us across the break if we can but momentarily suspend our disbelief.[5]

It is interesting to compare David's deed with that of Saul: Saul's achievement had been to rally his fellow Israel-ites and, as a conventional soldier, to lead them successfully in battle at Jabesh-Gilead. David's achievement is to overcome, singlehanded and unconventionally, the champion of the Philistines and with him the whole army. Again, therefore, David is marked out as enjoying the favour of providence in a most remarkable way. Moreover, the narrator goes to some pains to show that David proves himself in the face of Saul's impotence (and that of everyone else) and quite deliberately without aid from the king (17:38f.). The incident of the armour points up the fact that Saul's way is not David's way.

I have already observed that by the introduction of David into his court Saul has begun unconsciously to pave the way for his advancement. It is not, however, simply a matter of David's opportunity for experience as armour-bearer and courtier, that is significant. There is an emotional web spun around David in which Saul becomes enmeshed.[6] In 16:21 we learn that Saul came to love David greatly. Likewise, no sooner has David won his victory over Goliath than we are told (18:1): "The soul of Jonathan was knit to the soul of David, and Jonathan loved him as his own soul".[7] Saul's sudden eruption of jealousy at the public acclaim of David,[8] and his realization that David poses a menace (18:8), is thus vastly complicated. The struggle with David is henceforth conducted in the context of a love-hate relationship, and the story, inasmuch as it may be con-sidered a mirror of the human condition, gains immeasurably in intensity and sophistication. (It is worth observing, incidentally, that this important "family" dimension to the story is characteristic of many other stories in the Old Testament - nowhere more so than in the story of King David in 2 Samuel and 1 Kings 1-2.)

A crucial difference in the relationship between David and Jonathan, on the one hand, and David and Saul, on the other, is hinted at immediately Jonathan is introduced into the narrative (18:3-5):

> Then Jonathan made a covenant with David, because he loved him as his own soul. And Jonathan stripped himself of the robe that was upon him, and gave it to David, and his armour, and even his sword and his bow and his girdle. And David went out and was successful.

In 17:38f. we saw David offered Saul's armour and sword, only to reject them - "I cannot go with these" - in favour of going to meet the enemy champion clad and armed simply as he was. Yet now he can accept Jonathan's armour and sword and clad thus (so the following sentences seem to imply) he is able to go out successfully to battle! As Jobling has observed (1978:22), already Jonathan's future mediating role between Saul and David is being marked out. David can receive from Jonathan what he cannot receive from Saul.

What he will ultimately receive from Jonathan is the kingdom (23:17)! The symbolism of the clothes[9] nicely encapsulates and foreshadows this transference. In 15:27f. the tearing (qr') of Saul's robe (me'îl) is directly associated with the tearing (qr') of the kingdom from him. The robe thus becomes a symbol of (royal) status so that when now we find Jonathan stripping off his robe (me'îl) and giving it to David it is hard to avoid the conclusion that we are already witnessing, in anticipation as it were, the transference to David of Jonathan's status as heir apparent.

With 18:8, Saul's outburst of jealousy, we come to a second major pivot in the story. From this point on he becomes locked (unknowingly?) in a contest with the will of fate, represented by the "man after Yahweh's own heart", David, and from this point on the negative side of his character comes increasingly to the surface. Humphreys with justification speaks of the "disintegration" of Saul,

The Story: 1 Samuel 16-23

though I would not wish to speak of complete disintegration.
The remainder of David's stay at court develops the
themes of God's incitement of Saul to jealousy and madness,
of Saul's increasing entanglement with David, and of Saul's
inability to damage David's interests. On the contrary,
every move Saul makes against David only enhances his
rival's prospects. He makes him captain in order to get him
out of court (18:12-6) but with the result that David is yet
more successful, so that "all Israel and Judah loved David"
(18:16). He tries to kill him by proxy, using the Philistines
as agents and his daughters as bait (we are reminded of
David's proxy killing of Uriah, in 2 Samuel 11).[10] The first
attempt ends in failure - David, like the folktale hero,
succeeds in his impossible task - and Saul is put in the wrong
by having to break his promise. The second attempt also
fails and he is forced to give David his daughter. He is thus
even more enmeshed with David: indebted to him for his
harp-playing/healing and his military service, and tied to
him through Jonathan's love and his daughter's marriage.

His action also begins to drive a wedge between Jonathan and himself. Having tried without success to kill
David by his own hand (18:11) and by the hand of the
Philistines (18:17ff.), Saul then tries to persuade Jonathan
and his retainers to do the deed (19:1f.):

But Jonathan, Saul's son, delighted much in David.
And Jonathan told David, "Saul my father seeks to
kill you; therefore take heed to yourself in the
morning, stay in a secret place and hide yourself".

From this point on, Jonathan's love for David comes
increasingly into conflict with his loyalty to his father.[11]
The result is that his loyalty (hsd) is transferred to his friend
(especially in chapter 20), culminating in his secret
abdication to David (23:16-8). From this point on, too,
secrecy becomes a dominant motif in the story, until David
finally shakes Saul from his pursuit (chapter 26).
In chapter 18 the intrigue was all Saul's; now in chapter
19 Saul's own conspiratorial action sets up conspiracy
against him with first David and Jonathan, and then David
and Michal. At this stage Jonathan is still closely identified
with his father. His conspiracy is directed towards reconciliation and indeed he succeeds in making peace

between Saul and David, although, as so often in subsequent speeches of Jonathan, there is some unconscious irony (19:4f.):

"Let not the king sin against his servant David; because he has not sinned against you, and because his deeds have been very good for you. And he took his life in his hand and slew the Philistine, and Yahweh wrought a great victory for all Israel".

Given that what David has been doing most recently are "deeds" which have totally frustrated Saul's attempts to be rid of him we might have expected the king to be somewhat less than enthusiastic about being told of the "good" that David has been doing for him. Moreover, the phrase descriptive of David's defeat of the Philistine - "and Yahweh wrought a great victory (tešûʿāh) for all Israel" - takes us back to Saul's own initial triumph, at Jabesh-Gilead, and to his own words to the people (11:13) - "today Yahweh has wrought a victory [deliverance] in Israel" - thus emphasizing that David is treading the road to kingship that Saul once trod. But what Jonathan says was true: Saul "saw it [the defeat of Goliath] and rejoiced".

If Saul sees the pattern of his doom in Jonathan's speech he does not let on. Rather he acts as he acted at Jabesh-Gilead when the people demanded the death of those who had poured scorn on him and when he had ascribed to Yahweh the victory (11:13):

"Not a man shall be put to death this day, for today Yahweh has wrought a victory in Israel".

He "obeys" (šmʿ bqwl) Jonathan and declares (19:6):

"As Yahweh lives, he shall not die!"

So there is peace and David "was in Saul's presence as before". But Yahweh cannot have peace between Saul and David. With the requisite conditions for a fit of violent jealousy established by another of David's military feats, the evil spirit from Yahweh attacks Saul and so Saul attacks David (19:9-10). At the first attempt on his life (18:11) David had evaded Saul (sbb); now David not only eludes Saul (pṭr), he flees (nws) and escapes (mlṭ). The end of David's time at court comes with his escape down through the

82

The Story: 1 Samuel 16-23

window, aided by Saul's own daughter, Michal. The story is preceded by "And David fled (nws) ad escaped (mlt)" (19:10), ends with "And (so) David fled (brh) and escaped (mlt)" (19:18), and is punctuated by the same refrain (19:12, 17). The motif of "escape" will dominate the next section of the story.

Saul and his rival:
David at large (1 Samuel 19:18-23:29)

The next stage in the story is another that begins with Samuel. Now the prophet is openly engaged in helping the king's enemy. Once more we are taken back to the beginning of Saul's career, as the spirit of prophecy, which had marked out his election then (10:10-2), is used now to circumvent his purpose (19:19-24).[12] As we have seen already, the gift of "prophecy" is an ambiguous one. Saul is reduced to impotence before Samuel by being thrown into an ecstatic frenzy: he "raves" or "prophesies" (depending on how one chooses to see it). In the light of his raving/ prophesying in 18:10, it is clear that the spirit of prophecy can function in precisely the same way as the spirit of evil. Both are weapons in the hand of God.

His helplessness before Samuel is marked symbolically by his nakedness. We are told that he "stripped off" (pšt) his clothes and lay naked, as he raved/prophesied.

With chapter 20 the relationship between Saul, David and Jonathan is further explored. The episode with the arrows provides some dramatic tension, though this is not particularly well handled since the point of the arrows (secret communication without personal contact) is destroyed by the subsequent conversation of the two characters involved.[13] What is lacking in the manipulation of the plot, however, is more than made up for by tensions concerning the relations of the characters one to another, tensions created through both speech and action.

The role of Jonathan as mediator has already been remarked upon (above, on chapter 18). It is prominent in the present chapter. But chapter 20 also carries forward the process by which Jonathan's identification of interest with his father becomes less and his tendency to identify with David becomes more marked. The scene starts with David's demand to know his fault:

"What have I done? What is my guilt...that [your father] is seeking my life?"[14]

Clinging, no doubt, to Saul's assurance to him (19:6), Jonathan protests:

"Far from it! You shall not die! Behold, my father does nothing either great or small without disclosing it to me; and why should my father hide this from me? It is not so".[15]

Yet by the end of the subsequent negotiations Jonathan has only moved backwards; his father's answer (20:31) is: "Therefore send and fetch him to me, for he shall surely die". And Jonathan finds himself now demanding, as David himself: "Why should he be put to death? What has he done?"

In a sense Jonathan is on the way to becoming David. It comes as no surprise, then, to find Saul, in an upsurge of mad anger, hurling his spear at his own son (20:33), as he had done in the past at David his rival (18:11, 19:10) - Stoebe (p. 288) notes that the spear is cast "in effect at David".[16]

It is an irony typical of Saul's fate that his action only results in Jonathan's further identification of himself with his friend (cf. Jobling, 14). Not only does he "love" David "as his own soul"; now for the first time we see him in anger - against his own father. Jonathan's "mediation", like everything else, ends by driving Saul further into isolation. And again Saul cannot win. While we may admire Jonathan's loyal commitment to his friend, the concomitant of that love is an astonishing naïveté as regards his own father's position. He fails to see that David represents any threat to his father and is accordingly reluctant to acknowledge that Saul actually intends David harm (20:1-7) - hence the facility with which he is prepared to aid his friend and, as the reader may see it, betray his father.

At the heart of his naïveté is a simplistic view of good and evil, seen typically in the following comment (20:13):

"Should it please my father to do you harm, Yahweh do so to Jonathan and more also, if I do not disclose it to you and send you away. May Yahweh be with you, as he has been with my father".

That Saul's attempt to harm David might be a direct result

of Yahweh's intervention, Yahweh's having been "with him", or that good and evil might both belong in the repertoire of God, is beyond Jonathan's understanding. The rest of his speech is full of awful irony, right down to the final invocation (verse 16):

"And may Yahweh take vengeance on David's enemies".

When we remember the narrator's comment earlier (18:29) - "So Saul was David's enemy continually" - and Saul's words to Michal (19:17) - "Why have you deceived me thus, and let my enemy go?" - we see that Saul's isolation here is doubly great. Even in the face of Saul's fiercest anger (20:30-4) Jonathan cannot comprehend the king's predicament.[17]

Jonathan's negative influence upon Saul is captured in the text in another way. His first meeting with David is an intense experience (18:1-3):

And Jonathan loved him as his own soul...and Jonathan made a covenant with David, because he loved him as his own soul.

Within the space of a few verses Saul is intensely angry (verse 8) and, with the urging of the evil spirit from God, he has cast his spear at David to kill him. In chapter 20, the conversation between Jonathan and his friend ends with a renewed expression of that earlier intense commitment:

And Jonathan made David swear by his love for him; for he loved him as his own soul.

Again within a few verses we see Saul bursting out in anger (verse 30) and hurling his spear (verse 33). But this time the situation has been cruelly twisted. In 18:2, in the midst of the report of Jonathan's love, we were told that "Saul took [David] that day, and would not let him return to his father's house". In chapter 20 the issue is David's absence from Saul's house, but this time, ironically, there is more than a dark hint that Saul wants David's presence only so as to be in a position to kill him. In chapter 18 Saul's anger is first kindled at the song of praise for David and Saul by the women who go to meet the victors; in chapter 20 it is anger at the attempted justification against Saul by his own son. And, as we have observed, his attempt to kill

David in chapter 18 is now transformed into an attempt to kill his own son. Saul's fall gathers pace.

With chapter 21 we follow the fortunes of the fleeing David. First he approaches the priests at Nob and taking a pragmatic view of his ritual obligations persuades (deceives?) Ahimelech the priest to give him provisions in defiance of religious law.[18] Then, with Goliath's sword in hand, he flees - to the Philistines! David certainly has panache. But this (first) time his visit is not timely; sensing danger he extracts himself from the situation by feigning madness. It creates a nice contrast. David controls madness. Madness controls Saul. As things turn out his cool reception at Gath proves a boon in the long run. Forced to escape to the cave of Adullam he finds himself rapidly acquiring a sizeable band of armed men, the power base which is to make him a force to be reckoned with in the land and which clearly makes his second visit to Achish (chapter 27) a rather different occasion from the first.[19]

With his establishment as captain of an armed force, the verbs of motion ("escape" [mlṭ], "flee" [brḥ]) become for a time less urgent ("depart" [hlk] and "go" [bw']). This sense of quiet consolidation is reinforced by the snippet of information about his moving his parents to the safe keeping of the king of Moab. Saul's subsequent action against the priests of Nob seems, therefore, all the more hysterical.

The story of David's visit to Nob is not without its point for Saul. At the level of interpretation we can see once again the contrast between Saul and David. Saul the pragmatist is condemned by Yahweh (chapter 13, and compare the ironic reversals of chapter 14); David the pragmatist finds only favour. At the level of plot we have another thread leading towards yet another failure on Saul's part - the slaughter of the priests (22:6-23).

The scene starts with Saul venting his anger at his discovery that Jonathan has "made a league with" David. He accuses all his servants of "conspiring" (qšr) against him by refusing to disclose the truth to him. (And did Saul, we might wonder, "disclose" his true intentions about David to Jonathan?) The accusation is clearly somewhat wild and the truth as he sees it is blacker than we know it to be: for he believes that not only has Jonathan made a pact with David but he has "stirred up (qwm)" David against him, "to lie in

86

wait ('rb) as at this day". David is contemptuously referred
to as "the son of Jesse" and his inferiority clearly defined by
calling him "my servant".

An evil genius is never far from Saul. Doeg the Edomite
cleverly deflects Saul's anger from the servants by offering
now his "information" about Ahimelech. Shrewdly he picks
up the king's tone ("I saw the son of Jesse...") and offers just
enough information - nothing about Ahimelech's cautious
enquiries about the propriety of David's request - to make a
damning case. An angry Saul needs no prodding. In a trice
the accusation he has just hurled at his servants and
Jonathan is now hurled at Ahimelech (22:13):

> "Why have you conspired (qšr) against me, you and
> the son of Jesse...so that he has risen (qwm) against
> me, to lie in wait ('rb) as at this day?"

Saul's world has become so packed with suspicion that his
suspicions are now indiscriminate.

Ahimelech's answer is rather unfortunate. In the
circumstances the last thing Saul wishes to be reminded of
is that David is his son-in-law and the captain of his
bodyguard. That is to add insult to injury. So again Saul
plunges into a reckless judgement (cf. chapter 14?), again
one that bears some of the signs of Samuel's judgement
against him. The priests must die, he says, "for they knew
that [David] fled, and did not disclose it to me" (22:17).
When we remember Ahimelech coming to meet David,
"trembling" (21:1[2]), we cannot be sure that Saul may not be
close to the truth. But crucially he is prepared to make no
allowance for either the exigencies of the situation or the
possibility of action in good faith. Prima facie the crime
has been committed and that is all that matters. The
episode thus (rather like chapter 14) parodies the scenes of
Saul's rejection, especially chapter 15.[20]

While it is hard to retain any sympathy for Saul in this
scene, there is yet a certain pathos about it, just because it
presents Saul in such a terrible reversal of role. His
isolation is also further stressed since none of those about
him will "put forth their hand" (šlh 't ydm) against the
priests, save the treacherous Edomite, Doeg. (With this
scene the narrator has increasing recourse to the motif of
"putting forth the hand" and indeed to the theme of "power"

(yd) - the question is increasingly one of who has the real "power" and into whose "power" (yd) who will be delivered.) Thus the king of Israel who delivered Jabesh-Gilead and protected the Kenites is depicted as having his own Israelite priests slaughtered, and that by a foreigner. And there is further heavy irony in the writing, as we can see if, as we read the climax of the scene (22:19), we also remember the circumstances of Saul's condemnation in chapter 15 (verse 3):

> And Samuel said to Saul: "...Now go and smite Amalek, and devote to destruction all that they have; do not spare them, but kill both men and women, infant and suckling, ox and sheep, camel and ass".

> And Nob, the city of the priests, he put to the sword; both men and women, infant and suckling, ox and ass and sheep, he put to the sword.

And whereas Agag was spared, in the one episode, to Saul's eventual discomfort, Abiathar now escapes, to David's considerable advantage (cf. 23:6); for with the magical "ephod" David has the possibility of direct access to information belonging to the divine world of foreknowledge, so that no amount of double dealing (the treachery of Keilah, 23:8-13, or of Ziph, 23:19-24) can do him harm.

The contrast with the earlier Saul is furthered with David's triumph at Keilah, rescuing the city from the oppression of the Philistines, echoing Saul's deliverance of Jabesh-Gilead from the oppression of the Ammonites. There are various interesting differences between the scenes. In chapter 11 the initiation of the episode is caused by the "spirit of God" coming mightily upon Saul and later by the "dread of Yahweh" falling upon the people. In chapter 23 it is a matter of David coolly consulting the oracle. Moreover, we might note that David is allowed considerable flexibility in his dealings with the divine world: the oracle gives him a perfectly clear answer (23:2) - unlike Saul's earlier experiences, especially in chapter 14 - and yet David asks again (23:4), in the face of the people's wavering. But he incurs no divine displeasure for hesitation in the face of Yahweh's clear word, for "lack of faith"; on the contrary, he receives an even more explicit assurance![21]

In the oracle in verse 4 we are told that Yahweh will give the Philistines into David's hand and this victory duly

The Story: 1 Samuel 16-23

transpires. In verse 6, on learning that David had entered Keilah, we find Saul proclaiming, with a naïveté that momentarily rivals that of Jonathan, that God has given David into his hand, and setting out to besiege the city himself. It is David's role now to deliver Israel (Keilah) from her mortal enemies; by contrast the king of Israel is pictured as setting out to do precisely what the Philistines had done! Far from having mastery over the country's enemies he is now in danger of identifying himself with them!

Yet the story is not content to leave it at that. The final irony is that the people of Keilah are prepared, despite this topsy turvy situation, to recognize Saul's mastery, not David's, and to betray their erstwhile deliverer. To another man than Saul that would have been an amazing stroke of good fortune. To Saul it is more apparent than real. David, of course, is allowed to escape, by divine decree.

David now retreats into the wilderness, and it is in the next major segment of the story (chapters 24ff.) while David is in the wilderness, that Saul reaches his lowest ebb, finds, so to speak, his own wilderness. In the remainder of the chapter there are three brief scenes that mark the end of a major phase in the story.

First (verses 15-8), the extent to which Saul's position as a king with dynastic prospects has disintegrated is brought sharply into focus with Jonathan's further movement towards David's position (23:16-8):

"Fear not! For the hand of Saul my father shall not find you; you shall be king over Israel, and I shall be next to you: Saul my father also knows this". And the two of them made a covenant before Yahweh.

Though there is still naïveté here ("and I shall be next to you"), the covenant with David is made with an awareness, at least, of the real challenge to Saul that David represents. The last clause of the speech is also significant: it gives us a strong hint that Saul is near the end of his tether, ready to capitulate. With his conscious espousal of David's cause, Jonathan ceases to have any distinct function in the story (cf. Jobling, 1978) and disappears from sight, to reappear only in death alongside not his friend but his father.

Second (verses 19-24), the extent of Saul's loss of

perspective is indicated by the willingness of the Ziphites to betray David. Possibly the inhabitants of Keilah made their decision partly in fear for their homes (cf. 23:10), but the Ziphites arrive unprompted at Gibeah, keen for betrayal. We cannot help remembering that, but a short while before, Saul was accusing everyone of treachery towards him. In fact, as chapter 23 makes clear, apart from his own son, his own countrymen are all on his side, prepared to give up David and demonstrate their loyalty to the king. It is not treachery that defeats Saul but the will of Yahweh.

Third (verses 24-9 [24:1]), the irony of Saul's fate is once more thrust at us in the story of David in the wilderness of Maon.[22] This time he is nearly caught - so much so that the name of the place was called thereafter the Rock of Escape. Who should be instrumental, this time, in calling off the pursuit, just as Saul and his men were "closing in on David and his men to capture them"? Why, none other than the Philistines!

Chapter Six
THE STORY: 1 SAMUEL 24 - 2 SAMUEL 2

Saul and his rival:
Failure (1 Samuel 24-27:4)

The story now enters a new stage: the roles of pursuer and pursued are reversed. Two rather similar episodes with Saul falling into David's hand (chapters 24 and 26) frame a picture of David as an aggressively successful outlaw captain, winning booty and wives and making inroads of power into Judah itself (chapter 25). And at every point fate deals to David the right cards, the wrong ones to Saul.

In chapter 24 the action is narrated within the space of a few verses. The tension inherent in the situation - Saul helpless, exposed (!), in the cave; David's men eager to take advantage of a golden opportunity to rid themselves of their enemy - is nicely manipulated. Momentarily there is added tension, as David, we are told, "arose and cut off..." - but it is not Saul's head that is severed, but the "skirt" of his robe![1] The bulk of the episode, however, is concerned with the verbal confrontation between Saul and David after the action in the cave.

They meet here for the first time since David fled from court, and for the first time David himself protests his innocence face to face with Saul (cf. earlier Jonathan's intercession, 19:4f.). It is an opportune moment to do this since it is only with the incident in the cave that David has had an opportunity actually to demonstrate his innocence. Thus while it is tempting to see this chapter (and to some extent the two that follow) as somewhat flabby, overburdened by a preponderance of rhetoric in the form of set speeches, this would be to miss the significance of the

91

episode in the context of the larger story. It is not just another David-adventure but the moment for Saul to be put on trial ("sued") by David, accused by his former servant - "May Yahweh judge between you and me!" - and faced (yet again) with an unbeatable case. The case, of course, has been long in the making; the incident in the cave merely provides the final damning evidence allowing the suit to proceed.

It is impossible for Saul to win. What has he against David but his suspicions, his jealousy and his anger? By all obvious standards, David is in the right. He puts the whole matter in conventional terms of good and evil (r', rs', verses 11, 13). What can Saul do but acknowledge (24:17):

> "You are more righteous (ṣaddîq) than I; for you have repaid me good (haṭṭôbāh), whereas I have repaid you evil (hārā'āh)".

It sounds compelling. The reader, however, knows that it has not been as simple as that. Whence emanated this "evil" with which Saul "repaid" David? The irony is, of course, that it was, at least in the first instance, Yahweh's evil. Is it then Saul's evil or Yahweh's that is being contrasted with David's "good"? - a contrast that seems so stark to Saul that he is compelled to cap his acknowledgement of David's goodness with a prayer that Yahweh should reward him with further good (verse 19). The reader, on the other hand, is wondering whether David has not had more than a fair share of "good" strewn along his path. David's own speech has already alerted us once more to the complexity of Saul's predicament. By his invocation of Yahweh not only as judge but as prosecutor and executer of judgement (verses 12 and 15) he reminds us that it has been Saul's lot to find himself cast as defendant before such a court - an unenviable position, as the ironic oracles of the classical prophets proclaim.[2]

Saul, for his part, appears to recognize that he is in a totally untenable position. "This day your eyes have seen how Yahweh has given you into my hand in the cave", says David, and Saul in reply does not demur at this interpretation of the event (verse 18), though it cruelly contrasts with that fond hope before Keilah (23:6 - "And Saul said: 'God has given him into my hand'"). So his speech moves naturally from the blessing ("may Yahweh reward you with good") to the real climax of the scene which is Saul's first public acknowledgement of David's destiny: "for I know that you shall surely be king" (verse 20).

The first protestation of David's innocence was made by Jonathan to Saul (19:4f.); it produced a vow from Saul (verse 6) that David should not be put to death - a vow that was almost immediately broken in intent if not in practice. In chapter 20 David protested his innocence to Jonathan and secured a vow of loyalty by Jonathan in return for David's oath (a nice parody of 19:6) that <u>Jonathan</u> should not die (be put to death) nor his "house" be "cut off" as David's enemies will be "cut off" (20:14-7).[3] The inexorable movement has continued. Now in chapter 24 David's direct protest to Saul produces an open recognition of David's coming kingship by the king himself; that recognition on Saul's part means at the same time recognition of the vulnerability of his own "house". In return for "recognition", David now swears to Saul himself, just as he had sworn to Jonathan, that he will not "cut off" the king's descendants.

There is still a spark of struggle left in Saul. He does not offer to abdicate (as Jonathan had done); the kingship will have to be seized from him. But the demand for David's oath shows that, for the rest, Saul is now completely on the defensive. He can no longer hope that Samuel's threat against his dynasty will be averted; he can only try to shore up his house against depredations more terrible than the loss of the crown that was its treasure.

There are some interesting resonances in Saul's plea that David should not "cut off" his "seed" (<u>zr'</u>; RSV: "descendants") which are worth a moment's exploration. In a sense, David has already done just that; he has effectively cut off Jonathan from "after him" (that is, from "following" him - both as obedient son and as heir). More than that, we have seen this "cutting off" played out as a sexual metaphor in the love between Jonathan and David. While David's heterosexuality - indicated, for example, in the stories of Michal and Abigail - offers promise of a dynasty for David, Jonathan's intensive and exclusive devotion to David is strongly suggestive of a homosexuality which in turn would represent a denial of Saul's dynastic hopes.[4] Thus in this sense also David as the object of Jonathan's love may be seen to have "cut off" Saul's descendants.

King Saul: Chapter Six

This sexual metaphor surfaces strongly here in chapter 24. Saul goes into the cave (mᵉ'ārāh) to "relieve himself" (lᵉhāsēk 'et-raglāyw). The very term "cave" has a potential for sexual connotation: it associates easily with words such as ma'ar, a bare place, 'ārāh, 'ûr, to be naked, exposed, 'ārar, to strip oneself, and 'erwāh, mā'ôr, nakedness, genitals. David and his men sit in the "innermost parts" (yarkāh: flank, side, recesses, extreme parts; cf. yārēk: thigh, loins) of the cave. Saul goes in to perform one private bodily function; the scene that ensues hints at another. He "covers his feet" (a euphemism for defecation; that is, he squats so that his robe falls over his feet and no doubt as he "covers his feet" he exposes his backside). But in Hebrew the term "foot" (regel) is a common enough euphemism for "penis", and the difference in Hebrew between "he covered his feet" (raglāyw) and "he covered his foot [=penis]" (raglô) is but a subtle shift in a vowel. In such a context - and with an appropriate hesitation after "and he cut off" (wayyikrot) - what attentive Hebrew listener or reader could miss the sexual humour implicit in David's action? "And David arose and cut off"...his head? his penis!? No, Saul protects his sexuality but loses only the "skirt" of his robe. Yet what of this term "skirt" (kānāp)? Kānāp is a "wing", an "extremity"! Several other biblical passages encourage us to suppose that in this term, too, there is the distinct possibility of euphemistic use.[5] So even with kānāp the sexual overtone may well continue. It is only when the kānāp is defined as that of Saul's "robe" (mᵉ'îl) that the story can continue on a literal level as one about the cutting off of the "skirt" of Saul's robe.

At the symbolic level, however, the sexual connotations of the scene, having been established, continue to function through what follows. At this level of reading, then, Saul has failed to protect his sexuality (cover his penis); David has stolen it and its potency is now his. In verse 11 he proclaims that he has Saul's kānāp in his hand: "See, my father, see the skirt of your robe in my hand". Jobling has remarked on the frequency with which David and Saul use the terms "son" and "father" in this chapter (p.22, and cf. Koch, 139); and indeed the use is striking. David has usurped Jonathan's sonship; symbolically he requires Saul as father in order for his future kingship to be (symbolically) legitimate.

94

The sexual metaphor now pictures David in the classic (Freudian) role of the son who has usurped his father's function - he (so to speak) castrates Saul as Cronus castrates Uranus. Thus when, at the end of the episode, Saul pleads that David will not "cut off his seed" it is not without a certain irony - for his "seed" has already been cut off! Yet the sexual metaphor also makes sense of this plea, for at the same time it has shown that the "seed" is firmly in David's power ("hand", $\underline{yd}$: verse 11).

But the $\underline{k\bar{a}n\bar{a}p}$ (penis) is properly, of course, the $\underline{k^e nap}$-$\underline{m^e \hat{\imath}l}$, the skirt of the robe, and the robe, we have seen, is a potent symbol of status in the story. The robe-tearing in chapter 15 - Samuel's symbolic demonstration of Saul's loss of status - is significantly recapitulated now. The robe of kingship is at last in David's hands, torn from Saul first by Yahweh's prophet and now, to complete the process, by the one anointed by the prophet. It is interesting to note, moreover, that in contrast to David's earlier refusal to borrow Saul's clothes (armour) in chapter 17 he now seizes the piece of robe. Thus the incident not only pictures David's restraint from physical aggression towards Saul (echoed in the insistence, at a literal level, that David has not "put forth his hand against Yahweh's anointed"; even the cutting of the robe troubles David). At the same time it confirms symbolically that Saul's status - as king and father (i.e. dynast) - is in effect transferred to David and that in the process violence has been done to Saul.6

The hint of violence is not confined to the symbolic activity of David; it is also present in Saul's speech, "For if a man finds his enemy, will he not let him go away safe?" (20:19). As we have already noted, Saul has abandoned his dynasty, but he has not abdicated. There is no invitation to David to return to safety. David, he says, is more righteous than he. David has let his enemy depart safely. Saul does not say, however, that he intends to emulate that righteousness or that he no longer regards David as his enemy. Not surprisingly when Saul goes home David goes up to the stronghold.

Saul's public recognition of David's coming kingship is the cue for Samuel to leave the scene. His only remaining function in the story will be finally, and at the eleventh hour, to reveal to Saul the time and circumstances of his demise and, in effect, of the transference of the kingdom. For that purpose Samuel will be summoned back from death (chapter 28).

Chapter 25 picks up the motif of reward for good or evil which we observed in chapters 20 and 24 (especially 24:17-9). Already in the description of Abigail and Nabal a polarity of good and evil is being indicated (25:3):

The woman was good (ṭôbāh) of understanding...but the man was churlish and evil (ra') of behaviour.

And as the episode continues the terms "good" or "do good" (ṭôb, yāṭab) and "evil" or "do evil" (ra', rā'a') will appear at frequent intervals, twice as frequently indeed as in any other chapter in our story.[7] We also find here the familiar themes of violence and status. While the episode treats the action of David only and not Saul, the king is continually the object of thematic reference. Thus Saul, though absent, is never far distant.

Hearing that a wealthy farmer, Nabal, is "having shearers" - which will mean a feast - David sends his men to take a share of the bounty. The speech with which he sends them is a model of the rhetorical art, the first of several such. It is to begin with a salutation: "Peace to you, and peace to your house and peace to all that is yours". They are to point out that Nabal's shepherds had suffered no harm at their hands and that they come on a "good" day (RSV: "feast" day). Only at the very end are they to indicate what they want and who it is who sends them: "Pray give whatever you have at hand [=all that is yours?!] to your servants and your son David".

There is a wonderful effrontery about the speech - or so it appears to Nabal. Despite its polite dress, the salutation, the request to "find favour in the sight of", the humble familiarity of "your son, David" (cf. 24:11, 16; are we then to see Nabal as another Saul?), the request looks remarkably like a demand for pay-out in a protection racket. David's men have done Nabal's men no harm and David wants a reward.

Nabal answers with marvellous sarcasm (verse 10):

"Who is David? and who is the son of Jesse? There are many servants nowadays who are breaking forth from their masters ('adōnāyw)".

So much for David's claim to "sonship". Of course, Nabal knows perfectly well who David is - he is David the son of Jesse. But the "son of Jesse" is nothing but a runaway "servant", and there are plenty of those about. This scathing dismissal is strongly reminiscent of Saul's sarcastic outburst against David in chapter 22 (verses 7f.):

"Will the son of Jesse give every one of you fields and vineyards, will he make you commanders of thousands and commanders of hundreds?...None of you discloses to me that my son has stirred up my servant against me."

Like Saul earlier in the story, Nabal refuses to recognize that David is anything more than a servant - whereas he, Nabal, is master (cf.25:9, 14). That may prompt a wry smile from the reader, who has come straight from the scene of Saul's recognition that David is in fact a future king. Yet Nabal's response is not unprincipled even if it looks like being unwise (to say the least) in practice.

His shepherds certainly think it unwise. They hastily approach Abigail seeking help. Nabal, it appears, is a stiff, unyielding person. Clearly he totally disapproves of David's life-style and his servants know that it will be impossible to talk him around ("he is so ill-natured [a 'son of Belial']8 that one cannot speak to him", 25:17). Yet they also know that to rebuff David is to invite drastic retribution ("for evil [hārā'āh] is determined against our master and against all his house", 25:17) - a most interesting sidelight on David's character which the narrator has confirmed in verses 12f. David's response to the rebuff has been, without further discussion, to initiate violent action against Nabal (verse 13; note the repetition of "sword"):

And David said to his men: "Every man to his sword!" And every man girded on his sword; David also girded on his sword.

Nabal's servants obviously find Abigail a much more flexible proposition than their master. They give her an account of their predicament, and we do well to observe some subtle shifts of emphasis in the picture. David's men had been sent, the servants say, as messengers to "bless" (lebārēk; RSV: "salute") their master and he merely railed at them. No mention is made of the demand for "whatever you have at hand"; the mission was merely one of friendly salutation. Moreover the claim that David's men had done them no harm while out in the fields and that they had "missed nothing" during that time is now put in a slightly more positive light by the sentences that precede and follow: David's men were positively "good" and "a wall" (against other souces of harm?). Thus, though the speech is still suspiciously vague about the nature of the "protection" it does offer the possibility of a different perspective from that which had confronted Nabal. Are Nabal's servants really recalling a genuine favour or merely dressing up a racket in the interests of practical survival? We simply cannot be sure. All we can know is that the speech proves effective. Abigail needs no further prompting. Without word to Nabal she lays hold of a sizeable quantity of provisions and sets out to intercept David.

David is still breathing violence. He has "kept" (šmr; RSV: "guarded") all that "this fellow" (hazzeh - David's equivalent for Nabal's "son of Jesse") had in the wilderness and "nothing was missed of all that belonged to him". By refusing to offer provisions, Nabal has returned him "evil for good" (rā'āh taḥat ṭôbāh; cf. 24:17f.). Again there is a veil over the precise nature of the activity in the wilderness. "Kept" from what? "Watched over" against what "harm"? Had Nabal asked for protection? Just how "good" was this "good"? And, even more to the point, how "evil" was the "evil"? Did it really warrant wiping out Nabal and his household? Is David, then, to do to Nabal what Saul in his jealous anger had done to the priest of Nob? The narrator having prompted such questions at this stage opens the way for Abigail's plea to David to restrain himself from bloodguilt.

Abigail bows to the ground before David. The last time such obeisance occurred in the story was David before Saul, after sparing him at En-Gedi; and it was followed, we may remember, by an elaborate piece of self-justification concerning his refusal to do violence to Saul despite Saul's having done him "evil" - "evil" in the form of actually pursuing him with intent to kill. The contrast is considerable (cf. Levenson, 23). Now David is threatening to wipe out Nabal and his male servants merely because

The Story: 1 Samuel 24 - 2 Samuel 2

Nabal has refused to reward him for a service he never asked for. Or, taking his refusal at the level of "status", for refusing to recognize David as more than a mere "servant". Abigail's speech is a model of tact. She strikes the right note from the beginning: "Upon me alone, my master ('adōnî) be the guilt!" For Nabal, David is "servant"; for Abigail, he is "master". Indeed within a few sentences she is formulating an oath (note the stress on "life" and "living" here and in the speech as a whole) which parallels David with Yahweh himself (verse 26): "Now then my master, as Yahweh lives, and as your soul lives...." The phrase should strike a jarring cord with us; the speech is over-full, it is flattery, it is designed to persuade; it should not be taken at face value.

The vein of flattery continues (verse 28):

"Yahweh will certainly make my master a sure house, because my master is fighting the battles of Yahweh and evil (ra'ah) will not be found in you as long as you live".

But what battles is the "master" fighting? Right now he is proposing an onslaught on a farmer and his shepherds - a somewhat less than heroic "battle of Yahweh".

At the centre of the speech the gift ("blessing" - cf. 25:14) is offered, with almost studied casualness. Built around it, however, is an important theme (verses 26, 29):

"Let your enemies and those who seek to do evil to my master be as Nabal".

"If men rise up to pursue you and to seek your life, the life of my master shall be bound in the bundle of the living in the care of Yahweh your God; and the lives of your enemies he shall sling out as from the hollow of a sling".

Here we have the culmination of that series of imprecations against David's enemies begun by Jonathan. To the reader, of course, the primary referent is Saul. In the context of the speech the curse in verse 26 is that David's enemies should be "foolish", as Nabal (a play on the name which may be taken to mean "foolish");[9] but in the context of the whole episode the curse is more potent, for Nabal is struck dead. Verse 29 also functions as a curse, I

think, though strictly speaking it is not so grammatically.
The lives of David's enemies shall be "slung out" by Yahweh:
the metaphor is complex but the final image of the sling
brings clearly to mind the fate of David's first enemy,
Goliath. Lest there should be any doubt about the referent
of the curse here the language dispels it: for it is
quintessentially Saul who has "pursued" (rdp) David and
"sought his life" (bqš npš). Thus one of the important
functions of Abigail's speech, in the context of the story as
a whole, is to foreshadow Saul's death. Her curses pick up
the unconscious irony in Jonathan's earlier imprecation
against David's enemies (20:15f.: "And may Yahweh take
vengeance on David's enemies") and make plain that it is the
life of these enemies that is at stake.

Amongst the closing phrases of her speech Abigail slips
in the last great flattery: Yahweh has appointed David
"prince" (nāgîd) over Israel - not "king", for that, from
Abigail, would be treasonable, but "prince", a word redolent
with sanctity and authority.10 What man, thus wooed,
could then resist the force of those last words (verse 31) of
the speech?

"And when Yahweh has dealt well with my master,
then remember your handmaid".

That reiterated reference to David as "my master" (whereas
Nabal who, in the ordinary run of things - in ancient Israel,
that is - might be supposed to be her master, is no more
than "this fellow") comes sharply into focus. Abigail
throughout has been looking to the future, holding out an
invitation.

Abigail knows how to look after her own interests.
Nabal's servants know how to look after their interests.
Nabal, by contrast, is indeed a "fool".

David's response is inevitable. He accepts Abigail's
present, grants her petition and sends her back "in peace".

We follow her back to Nabal who is now holding a feast -
the feast of the things he had held back from David; and the
feast is "like the feast of a king". That phrase has a sharp
edge to it, for Nabal has not known that the issue was not
just a matter of "servants" and "masters" but of "subjects"
and "kings". He has provoked a king, Yahweh's anointed, not
a servant, and he who feasts as a king will soon be less than

a servant - stone dead. The coup de grâce comes, we are told, from Yahweh (25:38). David receives the news of Nabal's death as notice of Yahweh's judgement upon Nabal for his insult to David: "Yahweh has returned the evil-doing (rā'āh) of Nabal upon his own head" (25:39) Abigail is seen as God's agent in restraining him from doing evil by taking vengeance himself (25:39, cf. 32-3). Almost inevitably the final outcome of the episode is David's marriage to Abigail[11]- which prompts a momentary speculation. Did David spare Nabal and his household through his concern over the question of bloodguilt, or because he had already decided to accept the bargain offered by Abigail ("my master", "remember your handmaid") - his restraint for her hand in marriage when the time was ripe ("when Yahweh has dealt well with my master")?[12]

At face value this is a tale about good and evil - about good and evil people, and good and evil actions. Abigail is good, Nabal evil. Nabal does an evil action; David, a good person, is about to do an evil action in return but is stopped in time by Abigail's good action. Nabal is punished by Yahweh.

Scratch the surface of this "good" and "evil", however, and a rather different picture is revealed. These stark contrasts of good and evil are conveyed through some slippery rhetoric - rhetoric that is not necessarily motivated primarily by a concern for the truth. Is Nabal's death a just reward for his rebuff to what he sees as the "Mafiosi"? The narrative itself suggests not, not merely in the fact of Abigail's rhetoric, but through the contextual parallel with the slaughter of the priests of Nob. David is stopped only by the "lucky" intervention of Abigail from aping the violence of Saul. Yet Yahweh in David's place strikes Nabal dead.

Nabal is not an evil man. He is stiff-necked, a "son of Belial", but he is "evil of behaviour" (25:3) only in the sense that he is not "wise". Abigail is "good of understanding" in the sense of "shrewd". Nabal is indeed Nabal by nature as well as by name - at least in terms of the worldly wisdom that sets the standard in the story. He tangles with the wrong person. But does he deserve to die? It is the case of Saul all over again. The judgement against Nabal is not a matter of morality but of policy. As Saul is doomed to rejection for reasons beyond his ken and control so Nabal is doomed because, unknown to him, he stands in the way of God's favourite. To rebuff that person is to rebuff God – and the circumstances of that rebuffing, it would seem, are irrelevant to God. Retribution here is not decided on moral grounds.[13]

With chapter 26 we come back to the pursuit of David by Saul. Again, as in chapter 24, the episode turns the pursuit topsy turvy, though from Saul's point of view the second episode is an even worse reflection on the state of the pursuit than the first. At En-Gedi Saul had gone alone and by accident to the cave where David happened to be hiding. Now on the hill of Hachilah David goes by design to where Saul is sleeping surrounded by his army.

Learning of Saul's presence, David arises and comes to the place where Saul is encamped (26:3). Teasingly the narrative focusses first upon Saul's vulnerability to David – "David saw the place where Saul lay" – but then progessively lengthens the odds against any attack: for Saul is not alone; beside him is Abner; moreover Saul is within the encampment and, to cap it all, around him is the whole army! Yet despite these impossible odds David and Abishai go down to the camp. Verse 7 recapitulates verse 5: there lies Saul asleep, with Abner and the army around him. The only additional detail is the spear, stuck in the ground beside Saul, that spear which is a hall-mark of Saul. It is a significant detail, and the rest of the episode will hinge around it.

As if by magic (for how else could it happen?) the two intruders find themselves beside the sleeping king. Abishai imagines, as David's men had imagined in the cave at En-Gedi, that "God has given your enemy into your hand this day" (25: 8, cf. 24:4): "Now, therefore, let me pin him to the earth with one stroke of the spear, and I will not strike twice!" The irony would then be superb – that Saul should be killed by David's man with Saul's own spear, the symbol of his authority, and in the manner in which he, for his part, had sought to kill David ("let me pin him with my spear to the earth"; cf 18:10f.: "and Saul cast his spear, for he thought, 'I will pin David to the wall'").

But David responds as we expect. No, he says,

102

"for who can put forth his hand against Yahweh's anointed and be guiltless? As Yahweh lives, Yahweh will smite him".

The last person Yahweh smote (ngp) was Nabal, who crossed Yahweh's anointed. That thought is interesting for in the light of it David's rhetorical question is no longer simply an expression of forbearance, as if to say, "I cannot put forth my hand against him for that is Yahweh's prerogative". It is that, but more than that it is nuanced with menace, since it offers the precise reason why Yahweh will smite Saul. Saul is Yahweh's anointed; but then how much more is David Yahweh's anointed; and who has "put forth his hand against" David if not Saul? If Nabal is smitten by Yahweh for rebuffing his anointed, how much more will he smite Saul who has relentlessly pursued that anointed, "seeking his life"?

Suddenly, therefore, despite David's forbearance, Saul's death is close and almost tangible. David sees it variously: he will be "smitten" by Yahweh (with a "stroke"?), or he will just "die" (that is to say, before his time), or he will "go down into battle and perish". So here we have our first glimpse of Saul's ultimate fate. It is almost as though David has been unconsciously weaving a spell of death over the sleeping king.

In place of the king's life - so confidently placed in the hands of Yahweh - David and Abishai take the spear and a jug of water (a staple and symbol of life) and depart. The magic still envelops the scene (verse 12):

No man saw it, or knew it, nor did any awake; for they were all asleep, because a deep sleep from Yahweh had fallen upon them.

The aftermath of the incursion into the camp is first an amusing scene between David and Abner, and then a scene of some pathos between David and Saul. First, David calls to the army and to Abner (26:14): "Will you not answer, Abner?" Abner answers, "Who are you that calls to the king?" For Abner, to disturb the king's right-hand man is to disturb the king; for David who has just walked right past him to the king, he is no king nor even a general. With a sarcasm that will momentarily be hidden to Abner he replies: "Are you not a man [a real man!]? Who is like you in Israel [a man beyond compare!]?" Then savagely he

103

deflates the general: "Why then have you not kept watch over your master, the king?" He has not even guarded the king - he is <u>merely</u> a man, certainly no king, and as the man responsible for the safety of Yahweh's anointed he deserves to die.[14] We hear nothing more from Abner!

Saul now calls out to David, "Is this your voice, my son, David?" David replies, "It is my voice, my master, O king". There has been a subtle shift since chapter 24. In chapter 24, too, Saul addressed David as "son", but whereas there David addressed Saul in return as "father" as well as "king", now he replies, "It is my voice, my master, O king". Twice more Saul speaks to David as "my son", but throughout his own speeches David coolly addresses himself to his "master", "the king". A shift in their relationship has occurred. Saul is grasping at straws. Having acknowledged David as heir (24:20), David's "sonship" offers him at least the shadow of a dynasty. David, however, has now the kingdom firmly in his grasp, acknowledged by the king. He no longer needs Saul as "father"; on the contrary, he is now anxious to distance himself from the rejected of Yahweh; Saul to him is now simply the <u>king</u> who has designated him legitimate successor.

The coolness of address is matched by the heat of his protest to Saul. He shifts his accusation from unjust killing to committing sacrilege: the pursuit is a crime against Yahweh for it is tantamount to forcing David to "go and serve other gods" (note the foreshadowing of chapter 27, David's settlement in Philistia). Saul is forcing David to break the first and greatest commandment! This accusation is rhetorically clothed in such a way as to allow David, in (apparent) humility, to give a nod to the possibility that Saul's pursuit may be justified, while in fact directing the force of his attack (and yet another curse) against Saul himself (verse 19):

> "If it is Yahweh who has stirred you up against me,[15] may he accept an offering; but if it is men, may they be cursed before Yahweh, for they have driven me out this day that I should have no share in the heritage of Yahweh, saying 'Go, serve other gods'".

Yet for the reader David's (rhetorical) question is not so

easily answered as David appears to believe. It <u>was</u> Yahweh who stirred up Saul against David. If Saul is forcing David to commit a crime against Yahweh, then it is, indirectly, Yahweh's own doing.

Saul's response also takes us back to the Saul of earlier days, to Saul replying to Samuel's accusation in chapter 15 (26:21, cf.15:24f.):

"I have sinned; return, my son David, for I will not again do you harm (evil)".

"I have sinned....Now therefore, I pray, pardon my sin, and return with me, that I may worship Yahweh".

He continues now with an even greater expression of self-denigration :

"I will not again do you harm, because my life was precious in you eyes this day. Behold, I have played the fool and erred exceedingly".

Once before there had come a point at which peace seemed to be a possibility between Saul and David, only to be broken by the evil spirit of Yahweh (19:6-10); now we sense in the strength of Saul's self-abasement the possibility of a genuine offer of reconciliation. If so, it is short-lived - at David's choosing. His reply is to offer the spear back - but let one of the soldiers come and fetch it! He does not offer to bring it back himself. His speech resorts again to self-justification. There is no hint of recognition of Saul's abasement or acceptance of Saul's apology (verses 23f.).

"Yahweh rewards every man for his righteousness and his faithfulness; for Yahweh gave you into my hand today, and I would not put forth my hand against Yahweh's anointed. Behold, as your life was precious this day in my sight, so may my life be precious in the sight of Yahweh, and may he deliver me out of all tribulation".

Far from being conciliatory, the speech throws back Saul's gesture in his face. "As your life was precious in my sight, so may my life be precious in...." We expect a recip-rocal "<u>your</u> sight"; instead we get "<u>Yahweh</u>'s sight". David's reward for his restraint will be <u>Yahweh</u>'s protection, not Saul's; and the implication, spelled out even more obviously in the clause that follows, is that he believes he needs protection still - from whom if not Saul?

Against this reception, and as things are to turn out they are David's last words to him, Saul remains positive. If there is rancour it is buried deep:

"Blessed be you, my son David! You will do many things and will succeed in them".

So David goes on his "way" (for he is on the move, the way to the throne) and Saul "returns" to his "place" (for he remains trapped where he was; he has failed to escape). And what of the spear? It had been flourished by David before the king, but although its return is proposed we are not told of any such eventuality. Symbolically David has now taken Saul's place (and so properly retains his spear). The plot reflects this symbolic transference of power with Saul relinquishing the pursuit. With this resignation from his struggle to survive we are ready for the account of his death.

Curiously it is David who thinks he is in mortal peril: he now makes explicit what we sensed in his previous speech: "I shall now perish one day by the hand of Saul". His solution is to desert ("go over") to the Philistines. The news of David's defection reaches Saul, "and he sought him no more" (27:4).

Thus a cycle is complete: David had come into Saul's life in large part through the Philistines (chapter 17), and now he moves out of Saul's life through the agency of the Philistines. The difference is that in the first place he had defeated them whereas now he joins them! On the one hand this remarkable reversal can be seen as the result of Saul's persecution (Saul has driven out Israel's champion); on the other hand it can be seen as yet another illustration of the latitude allowed to the favourite of Yahweh. Without detriment to his status as Israel's future king, David can ally himself to Israel's sworn enemies.

Saul's end (1 Samuel 27:5-31:7)

Nevertheless, despite his new vassaldom David does manage to play a double game, serving his own, and Israel's, ends. As Saul had done so now he campaigns against Israel's traditional foes - "the Geshurites, the Girzites, and the

Amalekites" (27:8). The Amalekite motif is pursued a little further (verse 9):

> And David smote the land, and left neither man nor woman alive, but took away the sheep, oxen, asses, the camels, and the garments.

Unlike Saul (with the Kenites and King Agag) David spares no one; like Saul he brings back (but to the Philistines, not to Yahweh at Gilgal) the best of the booty - with impunity, for there are no finely worded hedges (whether of ḥrm or zbḥ) around his activity.

Achish is doubly deceived: not only does he think that David is out fighting Philistia's enemies; he also makes Nabal's mistake, thinking, "he [David] will be my servant for ever". As we know only too well, David is no man's "servant".

The speculation about Saul's death in 26:10 and his capitulation in 27:4 lend ominous overtones to 28:1, where we are told that "the Philistines gathered their forces for war, to fight against Israel". The focus of the narrative is still on David but in such a way as to have Saul always in the background. If war between Israel and the Philistines is to be the scene of Saul's end (as it was the scene of his first triumph) will David, as a vassal of the Philistines, find himself with his hand raised against Saul despite himself? David is in a dilemma which is only resolved, in chapter 29, by the lucky intervention of the Philistine lords themselves. The whole scene is redolent with ironies, one of the nicest being that it is Achish's trust (entirely misplaced, of course) that looks as though it will enmesh David in the coming battle, and only the mistrust of the other lords (David viewed as turncoat) that is his salvation.

These scenes frame the central episode of the section, Saul's consultation with Samuel. (The whole section has a chiastic arrangement: a. David with the Philistines, b. David against the Amalekites, c. David's dilemma, d. Saul consults Samuel, c. David's lucky escape, b. David against the Amalekites, a. Saul against the Philistines.) The episode begins (28:3) with brief mention of Samuel's death and burial, together with a rather cryptic note, the point of which will subsequently become obvious, about Saul having put the mediums and wizards out of the land (an act of religious significance). This is economical writing, sustaining the suspense concerning David yet introducing, with a minimum of explanation, the Endor episode. The Philistines have confronted Saul and Israel at Shunem/Gilboa. Saul is dismayed. The wording of this introduction (28:4f.) is notable, for it is strongly reminiscent of two other fateful confrontations between Saul and the Philistines, the first at Michmash/Gilgal (13:5f.), the second at Socoh/Elah (17:1f., 11).

When Saul seeks guidance ("asks": wayyiš᾽al šā᾽ûl) from Yahweh he is met with silence (cf. 14:36f.). Once again his subsequent action is triggered by the action (or, as here, the inaction) of God and a sharp contrast is thus drawn with the favours enjoyed by David. As though re-living that day at Gilgal, he takes matters into his own hands. He does what he himself has decreed is unlawful (or so the story implies) and seeks (bqš) a medium. It is the last time in our story that Saul, who for so long has sought (bqš) David, seeks anyone. The story is narrated with skill and subtlety (see Beuken's essay) especially in the way it conveys the nuances of tension, suspicion and fear in the interplay of king, medium and prophet, who is still very much alive in death. There is pathos in the fact that Saul should even at this stage seek out the advice of his long-standing antagonist. Above all we are given to understand the grip that Samuel has upon Saul. Samuel has decreed his fate in terms both decisive and yet ambiguous. Saul has spent the intervening period struggling with that foreknowledge. Now it is as though he can bear no more ambiguity. He needs certainty and is paralyzed without it. Past enmity is as nothing before the need to see the future with total clarity (again we might usefully compare Macbeth) and so he is prepared to humiliate himself again before the prophet.

Samuel's response to Saul (verse 16) is uncompromising - as we have come to expect.

"Why do you ask (š᾽l) me, since Yahweh has turned from you and become your enemy?"

But this time, for the first time, there is no ambiguity. Saul is a dead man; his sons too are to die (and so there can be no question of their succession); and the people (RSV: "army")

of Israel will be delivered into the hands of their enemy
(28:16-9; here the threat of chapter 12 comes to fulfilment).
And at last the time is fixed - "tomorrow". The implication
for Saul is that his life's achievement is to be blotted out.
Israel is to revert to where it was at Saul's first appearance,
blighted by foreign conquest.

The scene comes to a climax in Saul's fear (verse 20).
There are no heroics here. But another tone, of resignation,
is immediately introduced by means of the motif of Saul's
physical weakness through fasting (again the dutiful act of
piety before battle, reminding us instantly of that earlier
engagement with the Philistines, in chapter 14, and the
story of the oath). Saul's fear is real enough - sufficient to
make him collapse to the ground. But the narrator restores
his dignity by shifting the focus from the weakness occasioned by fear to that occasioned by actual lack of food.
The woman's rather motherly concern and the sudden in-
trusion of mundane incidentals - Saul sitting upon the bed,
the kneading of the bread - serve the same purpose.[16] We
are moved (with Saul) from the high world of destiny to the
ordinary world of subsistence. Saul eats and accepts life,
for food is the most elementary concomitant of life.
Jonathan had broken the fast unwittingly and found himself
condemned by his father for infringing the divine law,
against the protest of ordinary human practicality voiced in
Jonathan's speech in 14:29f. and in that of the people in
14:45. Deliberately now Saul breaks the fast: he signals for
the last time a willingness to sit loose from the con-
strictions of the sacral world. He becomes again Saul the
pragmatist, the Saul who was brought to recognize the
futility of a sacrifice of Jonathan in the interests of a rigid
piety.

In the light of Samuel's words Saul's action can be little
more than a token gesture. Yet it is typical of him that in
the end he faces life, even when he knows that this time life
holds only death in store for him. Without further word he
eats and goes back into the night.

Immediately the narrator turns back to David,[17] who,
as already noted, is enjoying his good fortune in being
released from involvement in the forthcoming battle, and
released, moreover, with blessings coupled with assiduous
advice. Whereas Saul's deception in chapter 28 has been

quickly seen through, David has been amazingly fortunate in his deception of Achish, even when pushing his luck to the very brink as in verse 8:

And David said to Achish, "But what have I done? What have you found in your servant from the day I entered your service until now, that I may not go and fight against the enemies of my lord the king?"

Then almost as rapidly as it has arrived the good fortune is replaced by ill: Amalekites have raided David's base at Ziklag and carried off his people. Even in this calamity, however, there is good fortune almost beyond belief: in sharp contrast to David's own practice against them, the Amalekites have killed no one but simply carried off all, wives and children, alive. Fortune lends a further hand in the "chance" encounter with a former Amalekite slave who can guide David to his goal. David, like Saul before him (chapter 15), wins a swift victory. The spoil is the Amalekites' undoing (as it was Saul's undoing), for they are "scattered abroad", celebrating their successful raid and the great booty they have taken. Thus David takes them unawares. He spares none within his reach. Furthermore he rescues everyone and everything that belongs to him (30:18f.).

Up to this point the good fortune of David might seem to provide a sufficiently pointed contrast with the obstacle-strewn path of Saul to more than account for its inclusion in the story. But there is more to the contrast than this. As already indicated, the attack on the Amalekites draws particular attention to <u>Saul's</u> Amalekite campaign (chapter 15) - and the circumstances of his final rejection in its aftermath. The aftermath of David's campaign (30:20-31) is most instructive: the remainder of the account is devoted to one theme - the spoil taken from the Amalekites.[18] As David carries off the spoil ("This is David's spoil", say the people as they drive off the livestock), lays down rules for its division among his own men ("it is what Yahweh has given us", he says) and makes "presents" of it to his "friends", the elders of Judah, Saul faces the Philistines and death at Gilboa. Samuel's words of rejection still ring in our ears (15:19, 28:17):

"Why did you not obey the voice of Yahweh? Why did

you swoop on the spoil and do what was evil in the sight of Yahweh?"

"Because you did not obey the voice of Yahweh and carry out his fierce wrath against Amalek, Yahweh has done this thing to you this day".

The arbitrary disparity in God's treatment of the two figures is nowhere made more manifest than here at the very culmination of the story. The thematic statement is plain. Good and evil come from God. He makes smooth the path of some; the path of others he strews with obstacles. He has his favourites; he has his victims. The reasons, if reasons exist, lie hidden in the obscurity of God's own being. Saul is one of God's victims.

Saul's death (chapter 31) is recounted in a simple, matter-of-fact, style. Perhaps the true climax of the story has already come, in chapter 28, with the last confrontation of Saul with Samuel. Within a few sentences we learn of the death of the sons (as prophesied). Then there is a moment of tension as Saul's last request, to be allowed at least a dignified death, is refused. But Saul acts typically. For the last time he takes matters into his own hands (quite literally now) and kills himself.[19] It is a fine ending, in the best "Roman" fashion.

Epilogue (1 Samuel 31:8 - 2 Samuel 2:7)

As Samuel has predicted, the battle is a disaster for Israel; the focus, however, is not upon Israel but upon Saul. The epilogue takes up two themes. Dignity has marked the manner of Saul's death; the inhabitants of Jabesh-Gilead, in an action of striking loyalty to the man who had delivered them from the Ammonites so long ago, see to it that he suffers no further humiliation in death.[20] The other theme concerns David, who now stands ready to receive the gift that has long since been his. Dramatically he dissociates himself from Saul's death and underscores his own previous restraint (2 Sam 1:1-15),[21] and movingly he grieves for the dead (1:17-27).[22] Emotionally there is resolution in the epilogue, particularly through the poem of lament, so that we are prepared finally for the decisive action of the closing segment: David consults Yahweh, goes up with his consent to Hebron and is anointed king over

111

Judah. Samuel's prophecy has come as close to fulfilment as matters for the story. The rest of the country (the north) will come inevitably to David, as is clear from the tone of authority and firm resolve of the final speech (in which, cleverly, the theme of Jabesh-Gilead - representing now the north - is neatly merged; 2:5-7):

> So David sent messengers to the men of Jabesh-Gilead and said to them, "May you be blessed by Yahweh, because you showed this loyalty to Saul your lord, and buried him. Now may Yahweh show steadfast love and faithfulness to you! And I will do good to you because you have done this thing. Now, therefore, let your hands be strong and be valiant. For Saul you lord is dead, and the house of Judah has anointed me king over them".[23]

Part Three
REFLECTIONS

I gave thee a king in mine anger,
and took him away in my wrath.

Hosea 13:11

Chapter Seven
SAUL AND YAHWEH

If the story of Saul is to be labelled a "tragedy", what kind is it? Is it a tragedy of Fate, or a tragedy of Flaw? The question, which was raised at the outset of the book, could be rephrased to avoid any suggestion that it depends entirely on one's definition of "tragedy". Does Saul fail as king because of his own inner inadequacy as a human being, or because he is brought low essentially by external forces or circumstances?

If my exploration has not wholly been on a sidetrack then I think that the answer is fairly clear.

From the moment of his anointing the future is loaded against him (in the form of the fatally ambiguous instruction of 10:8) and from his establishment as king in chapter 11 it is as though fate has become his active antagonist, thwarting and twisting his every move. (In this respect he is remarkably like King Oedipus.) We have looked closely at the key chapters, 13 and 15, and seen that his rejection by God and the prophet appears, at the most, to be calculated and contrived and, at the least, to reflect a remarkable readiness on their part to find against him. From then on he plays out an unequal match with David. Yet the demands made upon him and the obstacles placed in his path are conspicuous by their absence from David's experience. David is given a free hand and can do no wrong in the eyes of God, even when his action (for example, in his visit to Nob) appears no "better" (cf.15:28) than those fatal actions of Saul at Gilgal. David is "a man after [Yahweh's] own heart" (13:14). Whatever precisely that phrase means, the context makes abundantly clear that David is a <u>favourite</u> of

115

Yahweh. Saul, on the other hand, appears as a victim. For David, Yahweh is "Providence"; for Saul, Yahweh is "Fate".

The mainspring of Saul's failure, then, is depicted as the outworking of fate - fate which is in some hidden way the reflection of the will of Yahweh. Thus it is a conclusion which cannot easily be side-stepped in any moral or theological appropriation of the narrative by the reader. Nevertheless, the moral universe of the story is clearly not one of simple blacks and whites. Saul is not painted as any ideal hero. His attitudes and actions are at times tinged with a shadowy ambiguity, and although behind some of his most destructive initiatives (as behind the positive ones) lurks the spirit of Yahweh, it would be simplistic to claim that Saul makes no contribution to his own fate. The web of causality and (moral) responsibility in this story is complex and I do not pretend to unravel it. But I do offer a few reflections which my reader may care to pursue further than I have done.

Saul

The story makes much of Saul's jealousy - at times a desperate, insane, even violent, jealousy - and there are more than a few hints of rashness in his action, though the action most commonly cited in this respect, the imposition of the fast in chapter 14, can equally be seen as an expression of deep piety or the cautious exercise of kingly responsibility.

The motif of jealousy prompts comparison with Shakespeare's Othello where we see this mind-warping emotion distort a fine leader's perception of things and lead him to reject and destroy an innocent person, the one, indeed, who most loves him. The biblical story's treatment of the theme, similar in many respects, is yet significantly different. For example, Desdemona, the object of Othello's jealousy, is essentially loyal to Othello and innocent of the charge of adulterous conspiracy (though it is possible to play her as more ambiguously motivated in her dealings with her husband and Iago). Similarly David is shown to be innocent, though charged with treasonable intentions: he makes no overt claim to the throne, does not fight against Saul, and refuses to "raise his hand against" him, even when it is in his power to do so, and effectively at that.

116

Jonathan, the object of Saul's anger (anger which is triggered by his jealousy of David), is likewise shown to be acting in good faith, attempting to mediate between his father and his (as he sees it) wronged friend. On the other hand, both characters are in fact much more ambiguously placed vis-à-vis Saul than ever Desdemona is vis-à-vis Othello. Jonathan does, in fact, deal (conspire, make a league? - 22:8) with David behind Saul's back, and he ends by abdicating as heir to the throne in favour of David, thus effectively destroying Saul's dynastic hopes. David's position is more subtle. We (the readers) know that David is to replace Saul, according to Yahweh's plan, but Saul only knows that he, Saul, has been rejected and that a "neighbour" has already been designated his successor. Thus David, through his success as a leader ("Saul has slain his thousands, and David his tens of thousands"), naturally presents himself, in Saul's view, as a potential rival, perhaps the designated successor. Othello is fed by Iago (and "chance"?) a series of (false) clues pointing to a (non-existent) threat; Saul, on the contrary, is faced with (genuine) clues to a (real) threat. Thus his attitude to David poses a moral conundrum for the reader, for his violent jealousy, objectionable as it is, nevertheless happens to be right on target.

This brief comparison suggests at least two points which might usefully be explored a little further, namely the part played in Saul's fall by (1) his jealousy, and (2) his "knowledge" of his rejection.

(1) Saul's jealousy. Through his jealousy of David, and his consequent attempts to remove him not only from court but from the face of the earth, Saul only succeeds in enabling David to consolidate his position as a successful military captain and an independent leader in his own right, with his own power base. When Saul dies there is, bar the Philistines, no other power in the country. On the level of a political analysis, therefore, the story seems to be saying that the jealousy is instrumental in facilitating a course of events precisely the opposite of what Saul was wanting. In this sense, then, jealousy contributes to Saul's fall as it does to Othello's. But there the similarity ends, for the nature of each character's "fall" is so different. Othello's jealousy leads directly to his murder of Desdemona, and, on his

117

realizing his terrible mistake, to his suicide. The jealousy, the mistake and the suicide are all organically linked. Saul's death, on the other hand, has no direct link with his jealous persecution of David. Perhaps we are invited to consider whether at Gilboa, had the Israelites been fighting fully united, with David standing alongside Saul, the outcome might have been different. If so, the text only hints at such a possible construction; it is not inescapably a function of the plot.

We might compare another Shakespearean play with many points of similarity to the Saul story, namely Macbeth. Macbeth, like Saul, meets death in battle, struggling to retain his hold on the crown, against a foreign army. But the army is there on the encouragement of the "rightful" king, Malcolm, whereas the biblical story is at pains to show that David has nothing to do with the Philistine attack, and (again in contrast to David) Macbeth's other rival, Macduff, is in the thick of the fight. Macbeth's persecution brings the fateful battle and his subsequent death upon him, in a way that simply cannot be said of Saul's action against David vis-à-vis the Philistine attack.

In both Othello and Macbeth, then, the plot itself establishes a link between the character flaw (jealousy, ambition?) and the destruction. With Saul, on the other hand, the character flaw (jealousy) is linked, not with the death of the figure, but with his replacement, and this fact points to a significant difference in the nature of Saul's fall when compared to those of the other two tragic heroes. Their tragedy lies in the waste of their own lives. The tragedy of Saul lies as much in the significance of his replacement as in his defeat in battle and suicide. Saul dying of advanced old age and being replaced by David might still have added up to a tragic story. The death in battle, while certainly creating a dramatic high-note, essentially only complements the picture of a king who struggled.

The link between the jealousy and the replacement by David underlines the importance in the story of the dynastic theme. Saul's rejection is not just a personal matter but a dynastic one. In a sense, of course, his failure in this respect has already begun to be realized in chapter 23, when Jonathan assigns his status as heir to David - a self-negation

in favour of David shown through the plot to be closely
linked with Saul's persecution of David. Jonathan's death at
Gilboa - nothing to do with David - is in effect largely
irrelevant to the question of succession. With David's
coronation at Hebron this process of replacement is completed. Saul, therefore, is shown to be a double loser - for
himself and for his son. And his failure is so much the more
total inasmuch as his successor is the one man whom he has
seen as a rival and against whom he has pitted himself in
jealous anger (howbeit anger that is stirred up by God,
though Saul does not know this) almost from the beginning
(contrast Macbeth and Malcolm/Macduff).

In the sense outlined above, therefore, jealousy can be
said to function as a significant factor in Saul's tragic
failure.

(2) Saul's knowledge of his rejection. At the beginning of
this book I observed that it is possible to read the story of
Macbeth as a tragedy of fate rather than of character flaw.
This is done, not by denying the existence of (say) ruthless
ambition in the pattern of Macbeth's behaviour, but by
emphasizing the priority of other influences on the action of
the play. In particular Lady Macbeth may be pictured as an
embodiment of ambition who snares Macbeth at certain key
points in the play (for example, in the murder of Duncan),
and the witches may be depicted as no longer merely neutral
purveyors of information, which is to be used or abused by
the hearer, dependent upon his or her character, but as
positively evil forces who reappear in various guises at
pivotal points throughout the play (i.e. not only in the
explicitly "witch" scenes).[1] Read thus, the way Macbeth
interprets, and acts upon, the oracles can no longer be seen
to be simply a matter of his own moral failure; rather he
becomes to a large extent a toy in the hands of forces more
powerful than he. I say "to a large extent" because the text
of the play makes it difficult to remove all sense of
culpability from Macbeth even on this reading.

There is a useful parallel here with the function, in the
King Saul story, of the announcement to Saul of his
rejection. Has the announcement any link with Saul's
subsequent behaviour (the persecution of David)? If so, does
it have a morally neutral function or does it serve to shift

culpability from the king? That it is pictured as having an effect seems to me to be fairly clear. One example is in the haste with which Saul, who as a lad was so reluctant to be king, chooses to interpret an innocuous piece of poetic extravagance ("Saul has slain his thousands, and David his tens of thousands") as indicating a threat to his crown ("and what more can he have but the kingdom"), and in the passionate warning to Jonathan about David as alternative ruler (20:31). Moreover the hold that announcement has on him is demonstrated above all in the lengths to which he is prepared to go to gain precise knowledge of what the announcement means, in the closing hours of his life (chapter 28).

But how this foreknowledge functions, morally speaking, is a much more open question, just as it is in Macbeth. We can hold him wholly culpable for a violent and suspicious jealousy against one who had done him great service, and certainly no harm; but then, as we observed earlier, we know that his jealousy was nevertheless well-founded. And why was the possibility that another's success should be interpreted as a threat to himself and his dynasty so much to the forefront of his mind? - surely because of the announcement of his rejection. Moreover, the very ambiguity of the terms of that announcement (as it appears in both chapter 13 and chapter 15) - no names, no places, no dates, not even any certainty about whether rejection meant life or death for Saul himself or for his son - may be seen as a recipe for suspicion and jealousy. As in Macbeth the text of our story allows us to see the complexity of the moral dimension, the complexity of human motivation and action. Saul, one may say, is culpable, but...; and the "but" sends us back to look again closely at that announcement of rejection, its author, and its motivation. Thus by yet another route we arrive back at the role of Yahweh and the question of why Saul is rejected.

But before moving to the subject of Yahweh there is another aspect of Saul's knowledge of the rejection that needs to be touched upon. I introduce it with two quotations, the first from Soggin (p.195), the second from Jobling (1978:21):

> In the case of Saul we have a man who was elected by God for a specific task but could not surrender his office once that task had been accomplished and

could not see that others, more gifted than himself,
were ready to succeed him. From this spiritual
insensitivity there arose an inner conflict which led
the protagonist to pathological forms of mistrust,
hypochondria and persecution mania.

Saul does not learn who his successor is, but he does
learn of the rejection of his house, so that ignorance
of this on his part is refusal to know...; and wherein
can Saul's rebellion against Yahweh lie but in this
refusal to know?

These comments, while not making exactly the same point,
do have something in common. Both seem to find to be
significantly blameworthy Saul's active attempt to keep the
kingship for himself and his house. Soggin's attempt to link,
psychologically, this failing and that of the violent jealousy
and suspicion, though intriguing, requires perhaps a little
more demonstration from the text and explanation of the
psychology before compelling more than passing notice.
Rather what concerns me immediately here is the central
point about Saul's apparent refusal to accept his rejection
with equanimity.

While I am not sure that I have grasped precisely what
Jobling is arguing here,[2] it seems to me that by distinguishing between the rejection of Saul's house and the identity of the successor, and by emphasizing the question of
knowledge, Jobling indicates some useful lines of thought.
Is Saul's struggle with David a matter of acceptance (whether termed "refusal to accept" or "refusal to know") or of
knowledge proper?

The answer is not simple. Saul knows that he and his
house are rejected. He "knows", however, nothing else concerning either his designated successor or the appointed
manner of his removal from office. He knows everything
yet he knows nothing! He certainly does not "know" that
David is the neighbour who is better than he. David himself
is made aware of his role by Samuel; Jonathan is blessed
(but, as Jobling notes, not by direct revelation) with a sure
insight into the identity of the successor; Saul is left with
little but his suspicions. Why - to repeat our question - does
Saul refuse to surrender his kingdom gracefully? One simple
answer, therefore, would be that he does not know when,
and to whom, and how, he should surrender it!

But let us put the question a little differently. Does he refuse to "accept" the rejection of himself and his house? While the text does not allow us the luxury of being quite sure, it seems to me that Saul's concern for Jonathan's status as heir (for example in chapter 23) hints that he has not in fact accepted that Jonathan has no such status. That suggests in turn that Saul is perhaps not prepared to accept · his removal, or the removal of his son, without a struggle, irrespective of the question of David's identity as Yahweh-designated successor.[3] If this is right, Saul, in this · post-rejection phase of his life at least, invites condemnation (from the religious point of view) for a stand against Yahweh.

Here too an interesting contrast between Saul and David emerges. Elsewhere (1978) I have written of the story of King David in 2 Samuel in terms of a theme of "giving and grasping". David is at his best when he is content to let the kingdom be a gift by others to himself; or indeed when he is content to allow others their freedom when prudence might have dictated grasping them, unwilling, to prop up his cause (a good example is the case of Ittai in chapter 15). In our Saul story we can see the same theme in operation. David finds blessing (good fortune) in his careful refusal to seize what has been promised him. Perhaps, then, the finely constructed counterpointing of David and Saul raises the question, Would Saul, too, have found blessing by releasing · his grip on his kingdom at the intimation of his rejection? Does Saul picture for us the failure that follows a man's clinging to what is no longer his through the free gift of others?[4] One cautionary point, however: it is noticeable · that the people who asked for a king in the first place do not demand his removal. On the contrary, as was observed in the course of the analysis of the story, they remain remarkably loyal to Saul through thick and thin (contrast David's problem with the rebellion of Absalom and its aftermath, in 2 Samuel). Inasmuch as the kingdom is the gift of the people the gift is never revoked. It is only inasmuch as it is indeed Yahweh's gift that Saul can be said to grasp what, after the Amalekite war, is no longer his.

But if Saul's "refusal to accept" can function as an indication of culpability it can also, paradoxically, function with precisely the opposite effect. For the element of

122

Saul and Yahweh

struggle is one of the important elements in the composition
of the tragic stereotype. It is what sustains our interest in
Saul himself through the greater part of the story. See from
this perspective, the reader might ask, Why should the king
be browbeaten by the fulminations of a religious functionary
and the dictates of his inscrutable God?
    Here, then, we have an important element in the story
which is plainly ambiguous in value. Its moral/theological
evaluation depends ultimately not on the text, for the text
offers no independent evaluative judgements, but on the
stance of the reader. Is struggle against God (or "Fate"), in
such circumstances, positive or negative according to one's
own set of values? The phrase "in such circumstances" is
important to my point; for, as we have seen, the story makes
clear that Saul operates not in some theological vacuum
where simple and abstract questions may be met with simple
and abstract answers, but in "real-life" situations of moral
complexity and theological obscurity. The story allows a
range of responses to Saul's "refusal to accept", including a
significant degree of positive identification (by the reader)
with Saul in his struggle. This is not just because human
beings have so often had a soft spot for the underdog but
because the story in chapters 13-5 has opened up the
possibility of viewing Saul as essentially an innocent victim
of God, and thus of seeing God in negative as well as in
positive terms.
    Again we have come back to the nature of Yahweh in the
story. It is now time to look more closely at this subject.

Yahweh

    The story of Saul is about kings and kingship: the people
want a king, their God grants them their wish and chooses
one (we might remind ourselves again that the name Saul
means something like "asked for"); the king, however, is
subsequently rejected by God and, after a struggle, a new
king acceptable to him is established. In the process the
attitude of God to the institution of kingship appears to
have moved from, at the outset, open hostility or at least
reluctant acquiescence, to, at the close, acceptance and a
commitment which is seen at its best in God's wholehearted
identification with the cause of the new king, David. It
seems to me that Saul's fate is bound up with this transition
in attitude.

123

What are we to make of Saul's relationship to God? He is not God's enemy through his own choosing. His role as king is thrust upon him by Yahweh. He ascribes what success he has to Yahweh. He is remarkably attentive (almost to the end) to the ritual acknowledgement of Yahweh. Indeed both times he is found guilty of breaking a commandment of God he has done what he has done in order to honour him by sacrifice. He is prepared to acknowledge his error (whether comprehendingly or not), and even in rejection, worship him. Saul is not disloyal to Yahweh.

In Chapter Four (above), in the discussion of Saul's rejection in chapter 15, I drew attention to the theme of Yahweh's "repentance" and observed that the text invites us to consider that the story of Saul's failure is as much a story of Yahweh's "repentance" (which term, in context, clearly carries with it the implication of "change of mind") as it is of Saul's "sin". I also suggested that the nature of this "repentance" seemed to be complex and to reach deeper than the surface of Yahweh's stated justification in 15:11. "I have repented that I made Saul king", he says to Samuel, "because he has turned back from following me, and has not performed my commandments".

To be sure, Saul can be said to have broken Yahweh's commandments, at least on Yahweh's terms. But we have also seen that Saul's culpability is more technical than of moral substance. His condemnation (rejection) is radically out of balance with the nature of his "crimes". His explanations and the evidence of his "good faith" are conspicuously ignored. For a God who looks "not on the outward appearance" but "on the heart" (16:7), Yahweh takes a surprisingly superficial look at Saul's actions before "repenting" and rejecting him. Saul's rejection is not intrinsically and inevitably the outcome of his actions. Rather, God, given the opportunity (or perhaps better, having provided it for himself?), chooses to find Saul guilty. He is, so to speak, predisposed to reject him as king.

We observed above indications that Saul refuses to "know" (accept) his rejection. Here in Yahweh's pronouncement about his repenting of having made Saul king we seem to have a comparable phenomenon in mirror-image, so to speak. Yahweh is only too willing to "repent". He is over-eager to condemn Saul. It is as though, deep down (so to speak), he has "repented" already; now he is simply looking for the formal occasion to give expression to this attitude. Saul knows (formally) but does not wish to know (in actuality). Yahweh has rejected Saul (in actuality) but must seek an occasion to reject him (formally). The formal reason for the "repentance" is unconvincing, as we have seen. Is there a deeper reason?

I believe that the story does hint powerfully at an answer, and it is one that I have already raised in the course of the analysis of the story. We noted that there is a formal link in the text between the people's rejection (m's) of Yahweh and Yahweh's rejection (m's) of Saul. This is a useful clue. It leads me to make the following suggestion.

At the very outset Yahweh is depicted as a jealous God (a theme, incidentally, that is widespread in Old Testament literature). He resents the people's cry for a king which he interprets in terms of disloyalty to himself. Yet the status quo is clearly unsatisfactory. Saul, therefore, is kingship's scapegoat. Yahweh responds to the people's cry, but through Saul he "demonstrates" (perhaps to himself as much as to the people) the weakness of human kingship (about which he has warned): through Saul's "disobedience" the people, temporarily delivered from their enemies, are once again reduced to enslavement (which is the outcome of the battle of Gilboa in chapter 31). Thus God's initial hostility is vindicated and the way is open for him, freely now and out of his own gracious benevolence, to bestow kingship anew and on new terms (with a David, not a Saul, as king). The people ask for a king; Yahweh instructs Samuel (8:22):

"Hearken to their voice, and make a king for them".

With Saul formally rejected, Yahweh says to his prophet (16:1):

"How long will you mourn over Saul, seeing that I have rejected him from being king over Israel? Fill your horn with oil, and go, I will send you to Jesse the Bethlehemite, for I have provided ("seen"), among his sons, a king for myself".

First the people's king, then Yahweh's! Saul, on these terms, has no chance at all. Yahweh's "repentance", then, could be said to be rooted, from the very outset of the story, in his reluctant acquiescence in the institution of kingship. Saul vindicates God's hostility to the demand for kingship; David will justify the "repentance".[5]

McCarthy has argued that chapters 8-12 are centred around the theological problem posed by the institution of a monarchy: if Yahweh is Israel's king how can Israel have at the same time a human king? The answer offered by chapters 8-12, according to this understanding, is that while the desire for a human king is "sinful", Yahweh is prepared to meet it, though he demands in return the repentance of the people, the expiation of the "sin" (chapter 12).[6]

Jobling sees the succeeding chapters (13-31) as taking up a new problem connected with the institution of the monarchy, namely the question of dynastic succession (1978:6):

> Yahweh swore unto David an eternal covenant (2 Sam 7) that one of his descendants would always sit on his throne....Did Yahweh swear such a covenant with Saul [i.e. did he consciously <u>choose</u> Saul?]? If so, how could it be annulled [why was <u>Saul</u> rejected?]? If not, was Saul's kingship real, was Yahweh "for real" in approving it?

He offers an explanation of the way the story deals with this problem in terms of its structure and the symbolic transference of role or status from Saul to David, via the "mediating" figure of Jonathan (cf. p.11).

> In relation to Saul, he [Jonathan] moves between close identification and an independence which frequently suggests his replacing Saul. In relation to David, he moves between close identification and a self-emptying into David, a readiness to be replaced by him.

In effect, Jonathan, David's intimate friend, becomes a kind of substitute for his father, so that when he openly acknowledges David's kingship, he can be seen to be renouncing not only his own claim to the throne but that of the whole house of Saul. In Jonathan the house of Saul signifies its readiness to accept the legitimacy of David. Theologically speaking, we could say that in this way it is Jonathan who "justifies" Yahweh's action.

What I am arguing in the present book seems to be not

incongruous with these analyses of the story in terms of particular "theological problems", though I would doubt that these problems in themselves are more than subsidiary themes (of more interest, no doubt, to monarchical Israelites than to us today) in a story which has achieved more genuinely universal dimensions.[7] I have certain qualifications to make, however.

McCarthy suggests that the conflict between people and Yahweh over the institution of human kingship is finally resolved through the repentance of the people in chapter 12. My own suggestion is that if the story is read beyond chapter 12 then the tension can be seen to still remain. The people's repentance is only part of the quid pro quo demanded by Yahweh in return for his approval of the "sinful" demand; Saul's rejection (which can also be expressed as a function of Yahweh's "repentance") is the other part. Only when the people's king has failed completely is the process of expiation (the people's and Yahweh's) complete.

Jobling's analysis works well at its chosen, symbolic/structural, level, but I would suggest that character motivation (as opposed to structure or "plot") has a larger role to play than I think he has allowed. He comments (p.19f.) that in this story, "the rejected is bad, the elected is good, and to ask after cause and effect is pointless". From Yahweh's point of view (in the story) that might well be said, as we have seen. I am not so sure that it need be the case as far as the reader is concerned. For it seems to me that it is when we ask after the causes and effects that the story becomes most alive. Assume this programme of inevitable goodness and badness and the tale is no more than a theological tract for the times. I agree that Jonathan functions as a mediator, just as Jobling describes. But I would also argue that the transference of status from Saul to David is not just a matter of the symbolic resolution of a theological problem (the transference of dynasty from one divinely appointed house to another); rather the story does offer clues to an explanation of the transference in terms of cause and effect; that is to say, it offers an explanation in terms of the motivation and action of the key characters, amongst whom is Yahweh.

On my reading of the story, moreover, the "dynastic"

theme is closely integrated with McCarthy's theme of the institution of the monarchy (conflict between divine and human kingship), for the rejection of Saul's house, the fresh start with David, is readily seen as the outworking of that initial conflict over the institution of the monarchy.

With these qualifications, then, I would argue that the theological programmes McCarthy and Jobling discover are indeed there to be read in the text. But then I would want to say that these programmes can be read (translated?) in different ways. That is to say, in one set of (theological) terms, Saul's fall can be seen as part and parcel of the expiation of a sin, namely the people's demand for a king construed as the rejection of their "true" king, Yahweh. Expressed in terms of a story of character and action, however, Saul falls victim to Yahweh's resentment at an imagined insult (the "sin") and becomes the pawn (or scapegoat) in a process (the "expiation") whereby Yahweh vindicates his shift of attitude towards the monarchy and buttresses his shaken self-esteem. When we express Saul's fall in this latter way we may also observe that if it is jealousy that marks Yahweh's underlying attitude to the monarchy and consequently to Saul his (so to speak) supplanter, it is certainly the activation of Saul's jealousy against his supplanter, David, that facilitates Saul's replacement. The narrative hints here at an interesting continuum linking the divine and the human.

Read thus, the narrative poses its own "theological" questions - questions, for example, of rationality and morality in the divine sphere. At the level of plot, characters are confronted with decisions which involve the assessment of the relative importance of religious demands and duties over demands and duties of other kinds (cf. Saul, the military leader, in chapter 13). The judgements against Saul, startling in their severity, are made in the face of his avowal that his action had been taken in good faith. In the face of the repeated assertions of Yahweh's representative that he had sinned Saul acknowledges error and asks for pardon. But the text shows him reiterating his incomprehension and whether his repentance is also the expression of comprehension is doubtful. To Saul the judgements of Yahweh must have appeared as outbreaks of irrationality.

At the level of the reader's "overview", questions about

the moral basis of Yahweh's action are inescapable. If we are to condemn Saul for his jealous persecution of David, how much more is Yahweh to be condemned for his jealous persecution of Saul! And the question is one that lies before us in the story not only in our puzzlement (not to speak of Saul's!) at the judgement scenes but repeatedly, from then on, in the striking disparity of treatment between Saul and David. Yahweh manipulates Saul mercilessly, and he does so for what, on most men's terms, must count as less than honourable motives. He is insulted, feels jealous, is anxious to justify himself. It is tempting to say that this is the human face of God - but to say that is perhaps to denigrate man, and that is not something this Old Testament story does; rather we might say that here we see the dark side of God.

The disparate treatment of Saul and David directs our attention also to the fact that, according to the story, good and evil are equally at Yahweh's disposal. The story makes it absolutely clear that Saul's moodiness, his rancour, jealousy, and violence, are all provoked deliberately by Yahweh through the medium of an "evil spirit", just as earlier Saul's initiative in summoning Israel to Jabesh-Gilead (chapter 11) is shown to be at Yahweh's instigation through the medium of another (presumably good?) spirit. If the story is to be assessed in moral or theological terms then it is beside the point to dispose of the evil spirit by explaining it as a primitive way of speaking of mental illness (cf., for example, Mauchline, 130.). The evil spirit points unambiguously to Yahweh's manipulation of Saul.

Commentators can be surprisingly coy when it comes to facing this unpalatable datum in the story. Hertzberg (p. 141), for example, rightly observes that "Saul's suffering is described theologically, not psychopathetically or psychologically", but the only theological conclusion he draws is that "in an obscure way the hand of God invades the life of this man who, as can be seen often, exerts himself so much for Yahweh"; a little later, even the theological dimension is forgotten: "Saul is by nature extremely susceptible to such attacks in one way or another".

Ackroyd (1971: 135) comments more aptly, observing that

what comes to a man, good or ill, is seen as from

God....This raises difficult questions about the nature of God, questions which appear acutely in the story of Micaiah in I Kings 22, for there one of the heavenly beings is described as deliberately misleading the prophets to bring doom on Ahab (verses 20-3). These passages are not precise definitions but descriptions of human experience in terms of the will of God, attempts at setting out an understanding of what happens to man as being under God's ultimate control.

But his last sentence, in my view, unnecessarily blurs the sharp edges of the problem. We may wish these stories to be about, vaguely, "men as being under God's ultimate control", but on the contrary the Micaiah story says something quite specific about Yahweh, namely that he deliberately lies to Ahab through his prophets (at least the irony is choice, even if the morality is doubtful!). Likewise we are faced with a sharply defined difficulty in the story of Job where God tests, by afflicting in a most terrible way, an innocent man - and why? Because God cannot resist a wager and the temptation (by the Satan, no less) to justify himself, to be "vindicated". The parallel with the story of Saul is striking. Again, as in the story of Micaiah, there is another, positive, side to the story, for Job and God do not part company despite the harrowing experience, but there is no escaping the problem of the indefensible morality that assents to the test in the first place. To be sure, the scene between God and the Satan is "only a story", and it may be argued that it is "merely" a literary device to set in motion an account of faith in adversity, an exploration of the meaning of suffering. Yet there it remains, a picture of the dark side of God, so reminiscent of the picture we glimpse in the story of Saul.

We could go on. Crenshaw, in his stimulating discussion of the Samson story finds there a God who is a warrior, and one who delights in ritual purity (1978:133):

...ethical behaviour is irrelevant to this God, whose sole interest concerns external matters. Samson can murder and fornicate, and God will continue to bless him. But let him cut off his hair [a ritual matter], and God will depart from him.

130

It is no accident that Milton in his Samson Agonistes has Manoah questioning God's fairness (cf, Crenshaw, 145):

> He [Manoah] cannot understand why God punished Samson for a single error, when his positive deeds were multiple. Such dark thoughts are accompanied by radical questioning of the wisdom of praying for good things.

It is tempting for Christians to read the Old Testament in terms of what I might call the "optimistic" God of Christian theology - the God who is the embodiment of the absolute and the abstract, the all-good, all-just. The problem of evil has always been something of an embarassment in this tradition.[8] Of course the Old Testament is itself one direct ancestor of this view of God. But the Old Testament affords us, through the Saul story and others, glimpses of God in other forms. In the story of Saul, as in that of Job, we are at some distance from the innocuous God of the ethical absolutes: God can pour out his favour upon Israel, upon David, and even upon Saul; but he can also be unpredictably terrible, jealous of his own status, quick to anger and impatient of the complexities of human action and motivation.

Perhaps in the final analysis, even in this story, the "light side" may be seen as dominating the picture - Yahweh is early portrayed as the God who, in long-suffering loyalty, stands by his people and delivers them from their enemies; who is a shepherd, a bulwark and a refuge for his servant, David; whose hall-mark is good, not evil. This picture of God, familiar from readings which focus primarily on David (much of our story of Saul being widely known as the Story of David's Rise), is familiar to us all, and for that reason I have chosen not to elaborate upon it here. But the "Story of the Fate of King Saul" shows that God does have a dark side. David knows only one side of his God. Saul experiences the other.

NOTES
BIBLIOGRAPHY
INDEXES

NOTES

NOTES TO INTRODUCTION

1   Many have written more knowledgeably and eloquently than I am able on this subject. I mention but a few studies (in English) which the reader who is new to such an approach to the Old Testament might find helpful: Barr (1973 and 1976); Coggins; Kessler; Robertson; Good; Gros Louis, Ackerman and Warshaw. Not perhaps easy reading, but with many good things to say, is Martin Buss's essay on "communication". Some recent books that have adopted (in whole or part) a "literary" approach to their material: Crenshaw on Samson; Conroy on David and Absalom; Berg on Esther; Clines on the Pentateuch (note especially the chapters on "Method" and "Definitions"); Fishbane's collection of "close readings" of a variety of Old Testament texts; and my own book on King David (especially Chapter Five).

2   For a brief survey of recent work, see, for example, Hayes (229-33); for a survey and reassessment: Mettinger ("Part One: The Sources"); two major original contributions: Grønbaek and Birch. My dissatisfaction with the detailed results of such work usually has to do with the specific criteria used to mark out the discrete sources or traditions - criteria which often seem to me to be much too slender to bear the weight of the hypotheses that result. This I own to be a matter of critical judgement; many of my colleagues would take issue with my pessimism. No doubt, too, my own approach to the Saul story will be thought by some (I hope not all) to rest on equally slender threads.

3   In fact I suspect that the way I have defined the boundaries of the story is not too far removed from the way

scholars over the past hundred years have defined the postulated "larger complexes" in 1 and 2 Samuel, particularly the key one, the so-called "History of David's Rise", which when defined as running from 1 Sam 16 to 2 Sam 5 (as is often the case, though the details differ from scholar to scholar) cuts right across plain lines of connection with material coming earlier and later in the books. If one searches though the scholarly literature for the hard evidence showing that this "unit" once existed as a separate document one looks in vain. 1 Sam 16 to 2 Sam 5 happens to be a <u>convenient</u> demarcation of a story about David which does indeed read well as a relatively self-contained story (despite the connections elsewhere). So, I argue, does the story of Saul as it will be defined here.

4   And doubly so if we are to use the texts as historical source material - on which subject I shall have little more to say. (The interested reader might consult, for example, Blenkinsopp; Lemche; or Mayes).

5   For some interesting observations on the relative usefulness of "genetic" explanations (explanation by reference to origins) in Old Testament studies in general, see Clines, 9f.

6   The problems that arise in talking of the author's intention (in connection with much Old Testament material) are not dissimilar to those which confront the critic who demands a precise knowledge of the story's original social context as the key to its exegesis, given the paucity of extant socio-historical data from ancient Israel and the problems of dating and identifying the author(s) and editors(s) of particular texts.

7   In this respect (amongst others) I find attractive the assertion of the centrality of "values" in Miscall's paper and in Polzin's brief but pertinent response.

8   A close reading will note, for example, key words or phrases, parallels or contrasts in specific speeches or actions, larger structural symmetry (episode matching, or contrasting with , episode), the recurrence of motifs, the use of symbolic description or action, characterization and motivation (usually implicit , depicted through speech and action), the fabrication of tension and its dissipation which

is often linked closely to the manipulation of characters, and the identification of characters with certain values. The delineation of sameness and opposition is crucial, and here I share a characteristic concern of "structuralists" (cf. Jobling, 1978; White), though rarely, I think, can a story be simply boiled down to a set of opposing values without the danger of losing what is the story's own intrinsic contribution to the modulation of those values.

9   Kitto makes this point nicely in his fine study of Greek and Elizabethan drama (a book which I have reread with profit for it touches in principle on many issues which are also issues raised by the story of Saul). He observes: "The process of interpretation is an inductive one. The critic has to assemble all the dramatic facts he can see, and then try to find the conception which will best explain them. It is not a method which lends itself to exposition, since the business of collecting the facts, setting them down, and testing various hypotheses, would become tedious. For the purposes of exposition the process must, to some extent, be inverted: we must state, as a working hypothesis, the conclusion arrived at by induction, and show that it is confirmed by as many of the facts as the reader's patience may be presumed to endure" (p. 106).

10   This is the definition adopted by Humphreys in his stimulating paper on the structure of the Saul story, a paper which helped prompt me to explore this story further.

NOTES TO CHAPTER ONE

1   For the references in this paragraph I am indebted to Gosselin's interesting book on the interpretation of David in the mediaeval and reformation periods, which may be profitably consulted for further material. Cf. especially pp. 37, 46 n.55, 102f., 114 n.62, and Chapter Six, "David and the Embattled Church".

2   Some of the works quoted here are not exactly familiar reading in contemporary Old Testament studies. Although some may be labelled "pre-critical" that has not precluded their being of considerable value to this study, just because their concern for evaluating the moral and theological issues in the "final-form" text is also my concern. A few items of background information on the authors might be of interest (drawn mostly from the National Dictionary of Biography).

Thomas Robinson (1749-1813) was lecturer and vicar of St. Mary's Church, Leicester, for the greater part of his career. He is best known for the series of discourses on sacred biography (begun 1784 and completed in 1793) from which his essay on Saul is drawn.

Samuel Wilberforce (1805-73), who came of a privileged family and acquired considerable wealth and a noteable position in Victorian society, was for twenty five years Bishop of Oxford and later Winchester. He was much involved in ecclesiastical reform politics and tried to take a "middle" position, though his sympathetic understanding of the Anglo-Catholic movement earned him the antagonism of the Evangelical party. He was widely acclaimed for his eloquence, and used it on one notable occasion against Charles Darwin. A critic in the House of Lords once described his judgement of the famous Essays and Reviews as "a well-lubricated set of words, a sentence so oily and saponaceous that no one can grasp it", whence, it is said, he became known as "Soapy Sam".

Notes to Chapter One

William Blaikie (1820-99) spent twenty four years as a parish minister of the Free Church of Scotland, in Pilrig, Edinburgh, before becoming Professor of apologetics and pastoral theology at New College, Edinburgh, and, in 1892, Moderator of the General Assembly. Much concerned with home mission work, temperance and church extension, he also made a major contribution as a writer, and was particularly acclaimed for his biography of David Livingstone.

James Hastings (1852-1922) is better-known in Biblical studies as editor of (amongst others) the Dictionary of the Bible and the Encyclopaedia of Religion and Ethics and as the founder, and for many years editor, of The Expository Times. He was a (Scottish) Free Church minister, a notable preacher, in a simple and direct style, and has been described as being "puritan in temper" but "of catholic tastes in literature". His biography of Saul is perhaps more in the nature of a compendium, adapting the writings of others, than a homogeneous exposition; but for that very reason it constitutes a most valuable source of interpretational "tradition", particularly from the previous century, one which saw much interest in scripture biography.

Of Samuel Ridout (1855-1930) I know little, save that he was an American who also wrote a number of other books on scriptural subjects (Ruth, Hebrews, the Pentateuch, the Holy Spirit, etc.), and of the Reverend Clovis G. Chappell, also, I can say nothing (except that I believe that he, too, was an American).

The works of these authors represent, of course, but a selection from the rich literature of "sacred biography". One writer, however, whose work I read only after the present study was in its final draft, and to whom I would particularly direct the interested reader, is J.H. (Cardinal) Newman, who returned to the subject of Saul several times in his sermons.

3   Some flavour of this may be found, conveniently in the chapter on Saul (Vol. IV, Chapter III) in Ginzberg.

4   It has sometimes been argued that he was rashly violent in killing the "stranger" at the "place where three roads meet", but if the details of Oedipus' account of this incident are accepted they indicate strongly that he was

King Saul: Notes

provoked finally by the gratuitous and savage agression of the man in the carriage (his father, in fact).

5 There are interesting parallels in the case of Greek tragedy, where some commentators have argued that the respective roles of human and divine causality in the structure of events should be viewed as parallel but each self-contained; cf. Kitto, or more recently, Gagarin (whose argument - to me unconvincing - involves a denial that the early Greeks had a concept of the morally responsible agent).

NOTES TO CHAPTER TWO

1   So verse 12: wā'etappaq, "I forced myself" (RSV). This, of course, may be taken in two ways; cf. Goldman's note (Soncino Bible, 71): "'My conscience told me that I should wait for you, but I suppressed its voice' (Rashi); or 'I steeled myself to take this difficult decision' (R.Isaiah)."

2   But cf., for example, Birch on this chapter.

3   I am, of course, speaking here of the text as it stands; what might be the historical reality behind the existing story (possibly a matter of conflict over sacrificial prerogatives between king and religious authorities) is another question.

4   Another spirited defence of Saul - both here in chapter 13 and (unusually) in chapter 15 as well - is that by Gottwald (1959:180-91).

5   A more restrained accusation of impatience is found in Goldman's commentary (p.72): "There seems to be only one explanation; that his sin was that of impatience; he should have waited longer. The sin seems excusable and scarcely deserving of so heavy a punishment. Yet 'though it is impossible for a modern reader not to sympathize with Saul in his extremity, many times in the previous history of Israel "man's extremity" has been "God's opportunity" [quoting from Kennedy, 98]'". (Opportunity for what, I wonder? It is an interesting notion in the present context!).

6   See, for example, Hastings, 92; Welch, 76; Myers, 231; Blenkinsopp, 87, 89 n.54. Cf. also Ginzberg, summarizing Jewish "legendary" material on Saul (pp.65-72, and see notes 78-80 for reference to his sources); thus, for example (p.72): "So perished the first Jewish king, as a hero and a saint... Indeed, in all respects his piety was so great that not even David was his equal."

NOTES TO CHAPTER THREE

1   On "holy war" see further, for example, Weippert, Jones, and Gottwald's succinct survey (1976).

2   Text following LXX and many commentators (cf. Hertzberg, 121; Stoebe, 289.

3   Samuel takes Saul's reference to the people's action as a sign that Saul has failed to assert his authority. Good (p.70) sees this as "the psychological center of the entire Saul story": Saul is self-deprecating to the point where he neglects his true responsibilities as king in a superficial grasping for public favour (here through the display of Agag and the booty). Samuel's jibe encapsulates this factor of personal insecurity that is Saul's undoing. This is an interesting and in many ways persuasive analysis of a text (and story) which, nevertheless (as I shall indicate below), may be construed rather differently.

4   Note that the "but" (in RSV etc.) instead of "and" is purely interpretational, assuming a contrast between the two actions. The Hebrew can equally be read as I have translated.

5   The point may be raised that by offering some of the ḥrm-things as sacrifice the people were perhaps thereby enabling themselves, in a sacrificial feast, to partake of the parts not normally consumed, and that the prospect of this food lay behind the decision to offer the sacrifice at Gilgal. One cannot entirely discount this possibility. I can merely observe that there is no hint in the text of a sin of greed such as could easily have been given, even if only by the glimpse of a feasting, gluttonous crowd.

6   On the text, Grønbaek (p.60, n.88) asserts against Soggin (1967:56f.) that it is an insertion under the influence of chapter 13, but has little evidence for his view.

7 The clause breaks a sequence with waw consecutive by changing the order to conjunction + object + verb. It might be noted here also that hhrmty (perfect) could equally well be translated, "I shall have devoted...".

8 On such complexities in Hebrew rhetoric, cf., for example, Braulik, König, Melamed. Incidentally, the verb ("spared") in 15:9 is in the singular.

9 Cf. Good, 70f.; Hertzberg, 127; McKane, 104.

10 Similarly Weiser (pp. 8-14) argues that Saul genuinely believed that to bring part of the booty for sacrifice was no violation of the "ban" (hrm).

11 Where this complication is recognised, a resolution is usually sought in traditio-historical arguments. Cf., for example, Birch (p.83f.) on chapter 13: the material derives from a circle of prophets with sacrificial functions especially in the context of the "holy war". McKenzie sees this tradition (chapter 13) as in fact of priestly, not prophetic origin.

Ambivalence over the priority of prophetic word (and unquestioning "obedience" to the prophet, especially by the king) or cultic act (propriety of sacrifice, especially outside the "central sanctuary"; interest in the temple and its paraphernalia, etc.) is characteristic of the "Deuteronomistic History" as a whole, and were I to develop an interpretation of that larger unit this is a tension I should wish to explore. It is a commonplace to assert that Israel, in the History, is judged for her sins which are "mostly cultic" (Crenshaw, 1979:131); yet little attempt (other than by way of positing separate redactors) has been made to integrate this view of the prophetic dimension to which attention is increasingly being drawn (especially following Dietrich).

12 Knierim (p.37), answering the question, why is Saul's rejection "final", writes: "Yahweh's repentance is a decision that makes ineffective both Samuel's intercession (v. 11) and Saul's confession of sin. It is the real reason for the radicality of the rejection....Our text seems to contain a theology according to which Saul has miscarried not so much on account of his own sin but rather because of Yahweh." But if I am not mistaken (and I own to finding the essay a little difficult to follow), Knierim's direction of argument is

rather different from mine. He seems to be arguing that the finality of the rejection (the "repentance") is bound up with the fact that Saul is a "messiah" (anointed one) rather than an ordinary person and that Saul <u>does</u> sin (though what Knierim thinks the sin to be does not emerge with clarity).

At many points I find this essay (which I had somehow overlooked and came to only after my book was substantially drafted) correlates well with my own interpretation of the story, as, for example, when he writes (p.40): "In both cases [Saul and David] the signs and actions of the messiah are determined by Yahweh. They are not an expression of an independent ethical behavior. The elected can only succeed. The rejected has no other choice than to do that which leads him to his downfall....The messiah succeeds because of Yahweh or he fails because of him." But suggestions, elsewhere, of Saul's sin and culpability (cf., for example, pp.36f., 40f.) are not well integrated into such an interpretation; nor am I sure what it might mean, that Yahweh had "provided all the presuppositions for (Saul) passing the test and...demonstrated their effectiveness". In other words, the essay seems to me to avoid tackling, first, the crucial matter of the nature of Saul's "sin", and, next, the implications of ascribing responsibility for the "messiah's" actions to Yahweh, namely the implications for an assessment of Saul's culpability, for the motivation of Yahweh's "repentance", and for the evaluation of Yahweh's actions in ethical terms.

For an adaptation of Knierim's argument about the peculiar standing of the "messiah" in relation to God, see also Birch, 106, 148-50.

NOTES TO CHAPTER FOUR

1   This is another point where Good's interpretation and mine differ somewhat. He evaluates the request as unjustified (p.60f.: "The fact of incompetent incumbents is no reason to throw over the whole institution of judgeship") and sees the remark about "like other nations" as an ironical reflection by the narrator on the propriety of the people's desire for a king. I acknowledge the irony, but would suggest that it can cut several ways: if the people are seeking a king "like the nations": it is only because the existing "judging/governing" (špt) is in fact inadequate. Even if the apparently settled conditions achieved in chapter 7 (cf. verses 13f.) are taken into account (allowing a slightly different set of boundaries to our story) the beginning of chapter 8 indicates that a new situation exists in which the existing leadership is inadequate, and chapter 11 (the Ammonite oppression of Jabesh-Gilead) makes the need even clearer. And whose responsibility is the state of the "government"? Is it not Israel's existing "king" - Yahweh?

2   Cf. also verse 26 and 16:1.

3   On this "proverb" and the notion of "prophesying" see, for example, Ackroyd, 1971:85; McKane, 75f., 116, 122-4; Mauchline, 100, 144; Stoebe, 211; Wilson, 329-36.

4   Note the play on words here, which picks up the theme of "obeying"/"hearkening to the voice of" Yahweh: Samuel sends the people thunder (qwl - "voice"!).

5   'kr is usually translated "trouble", "disturb". See further, Jobling, 1976:370, n.11 (he defines as "bring into cultic jeopardy"); Whitelam, 78-80. Whitelam (p.80), taking issue with Jobling and McKane amongst others, argues that Jonathan's accusation against Saul (together with his lone exploits) indicates something akin to a conspiracy, "a direct challenge to Saul as king and commander of the army".

145

Whitelam's interests are historical rather than literary and, unless I am mistaken, this conclusion relates to "what actually happened" rather than "what the story now says".

Whitelam tends to argue from what he considers to be historical "probability" (so here) rather than from a sustained exegesis of the existing text (as Jobling). Such a procedure is, of course, perfectly reasonable in a historical investigation, but I believe he overestimates our ability to assess the historical status of the ultimate starting point in his study, namely the story itself, as we have it. Taking just one aspect of such an assessment, I note, for example, the judgement (p.81) that "The narratives [about Saul and David in 1 Samuel], as the product of a Davidic historian, necessarily portray a strong pro-Davidic and anti-Saul nature"; to my mind this claim cuts much too readily through a host of unknowns and complex possibilities.

6   On the text see Hertzberg, 110f., 116f.; Stoebe, 269f.; Whitelam, 75.

7   That is to say, having delivered them out of the hand of the Philistines, they might yet be delivered back into their hands (chapter 31). Mettinger (p.34) notes also that this verse seems to point forward to the circumstances of David's coming to court. I would add that on that occasion (David against Goliath) the reversal of the promise is already beginning to take effect, for it is then not Saul but David who effectively delivers Israel from the Philistines.

8   Samuel is not an easy figure to characterize. There are indications of the "human" Samuel (cf. 15:11 and 15:35), though even these are not without ambiguity, and certainly any personal feeling of the prophet is subordinated to his function as the agent of Yahweh. In 15:11 it is not made clear just why Samuel is "angry" and in what sense he is "crying" (z'q, which usually means "crying for help") to Yahweh. Does he feel, and oppose, the readiness of Yahweh to condemn Saul, so that he is interceding (z"q) for Saul (cf., for example, Hertzberg, 126). Or is he perhaps unhappy about being placed once again in a position of antagonism towards the king, so that he is asking Yahweh to relent for his own sake? Or is he angry at Saul, and does he pray (z'q) all night to Yahweh asking that he should finally and decisively give expression to his repentance? Whatever the

case, the point in the end is the same: "he must...fall in with the will of the Lord and agree with him" (Hertzberg). The sentence about Samuel "mourning" over Saul (15:35, cf. 16:1; RSV: "grieving") is double-edged. It may be read as indicating grief at the loss of the king; more to the point is the fact that the word used ('bl) is that normally used for mourning or lamenting for the dead. As far as Samuel is concerned, Saul is a dead man! Thus the sentence may direct us to contemplate not a soft-hearted Samuel, as the translation "grieved" might suggest, but a doomed Saul. (Jeremiah uses a similar technique in Jer. 7:18-23 to make an equally savage point; or cf. Amos 5:1f.).

9   The phrase is used eighteen times in the story of Saul: five in chapter 15; four in chapter 8. Other occurrences: three in chapter 12 (and see above, note 4); 19:6 (Saul to Jonathan) and 23:35 (David to Abigail) - both cases of "obeying" mediators who prevent bloodshed; four in chapter 28 - it is interesting that Saul's last act of "obeying" is to his "servants" (cf. earlier, for example in chapters 14 and 15, where he "obeys" the "people").

NOTES TO CHAPTER FIVE

1   This seems to be a common motif in the Books of Samuel: cf. 20:5-7; 2 Sam 13:23-9; 15:7-13.
   On narrative technique in this chapter, Kessler's study is particularly useful.

2   The tense atmosphere depicted also has the effect of conveying something of the critical importance of the visit, for the future hinges on this moment (cf. Gros Louis, 18f.).

3   Note that Saul does not jib at this; he stays loyal to Yahweh and does not let Yahweh's rejection of him force him into the position of rejecting Yahweh as his God.

4   Perhaps, too, 16:18 ("a man of valour, a man of war...") needs modification.

5   See Willis for a summary of attempts to solve the problem; also for a new suggestion which makes some valuable observations about the way 16:14-23 is linked with the chapters which follow. He has useful comments along similar lines on 17:54; 18:5, 9-11, 14-6, 28-30).

6   Gros Louis (p.22f.) makes a similar point when he explores the reason for the presence of the two accounts of David's coming to court: "The two accounts, however they may seem inconsistent, present us with two views of David at Saul's court and two views of Saul's relationship to David. In the first, he comes as Saul's personal musician, he calms him privately at court with his music and Saul loves him greatly; in the second, he becomes Saul's public champion, gradually, as depicted in the narrative, moving away from the private enclosure of his father's home, his sheep, his deliveries to his brothers, and into the public world of war and armor, visibility, wealth and influence. David has a private relationship with Saul the man; he also develops a public relationship with Saul the king. Saul the man can love

his comforter and recall the refreshment brought to him by his music; Saul the king cannot bear to hear the Israelite women singing, 'Saul has slain his thousands, and David his ten thousands'". On p.29 he develops the theme of the intertwining of the lives of Saul and David, noting that "the incredible tension and ambivalence which both experience is explained by the dual nature of their relationship".

7   Some interesting observations on possible overtones in the use of 'hb ("love") may be found in Thompson; and cf. Ackroyd, 1975.

8   The outburst of jealousy is prompted by the women singing, "Saul has slain his thousands/and David his ten thousands". Modern scholars have expended much argument over whether the elements in a piece of Hebrew poetry exhibiting such "parallelism" (in this case: Saul//David + has slain// [verb understood] + thousands//ten thousands) should be interpreted as "synonymous" (in which case the variations - here, for example, thousands//ten thousands - are for decoration rather than be taken too literally) or as "progressive" (in which case the second element is saying something significantly different from the first). One of the beauties of the parallelism in our story is that the poetry becomes yet another element of ambiguity thrown in Saul's path. In the event he chooses to take the variation "thousands//ten thousands" as significant ("progressive"); it might equally have been dismissed as of no consequence ("synonymous"). Nor do we know with what degree of mischievous intent (if any) the couplet was coined and paraded.

This incident is the first of a series in which Saul chooses to see David in the worst light (as, ironically, Yahweh has done with Saul in chapters 13 and 15!).

9   Observed also by Mettinger, 34, 39. There is a basic exegetical problem in the passage: does Samuel tear Saul's robe or vice versa? I assume (with, for example, Mettinger, 34) the former, but do not believe a decision on this matter radically effects the significance of the action.

10   Note the "chiastic" structure in 18:20-6, which emphasizes the fact that at the end Saul is no better off than at the beginning - perhaps even worse:

Verse 20.   (a) The thing [Michal loved D.] pleased him [S]
              (b) S thought..."let the hand of the P's be against him"
              (c) S speaks to D
              (b) S thought to make D fall by the hand of the P's
Verse 26.   (a) And it pleased D to be the king's son-in-law.

Note also the irony in Saul's speech to David (verse 25): "The king desires no marriage present except one hundred foreskins of the Philistines, that he may be avenged on the king's enemies". The reader knows that David already falls into the category of "enemy" (and the point is made explicitly in verse 29). The same irony is played out elsewhere in the story: cf. 19:17; 20:13 and 25:26ff.

11   Cf. especially Jobling, 1978:11-4.

12   See above, Chapter Four, on 10:10. Cf. Jobling (1978:10):"The similarities with 9:1-10:16 are so striking, above all in the repetition of the proverb, 'Is Saul also among the prophets?', that we should regard it as a satirical recapitulation of the earlier passage". Stoebe (p.368; quoted by Jobling) notes the debilitating character of the spirit here and the symbolism of the king's nakedness.

13   Such a minor mis-match of plot elements is not unexpected where a story is being built (in basics at least) out of existing traditional elements, scenes, motifs) as may possibly be the case here, not that such an explanation in any way diminishes the fact of artistic failure any more than does appeal to other kinds of "source" hypothesis.

14   In David's protestation of innocence (20:1), "What have I done? What is my guilt? What is my sin before your father...?", we may see a parallel with Saul's protestation to Samuel (15:20), "I have obeyed Yahweh...". (Note, too, that each protests his innocence to an intermediary who is closely identified with the "persecuter" [Saul's son, Yahweh's prophet].) Is Saul now playing the role Yahweh had assumed with him? If so, that is ironical. But the outcome, of course, is quite different in each case, for while Yahweh's "persecution" is resolved in Saul's death, Saul's "persecution" fails utterly, thus emphasizing again the different "fates" of Saul and his rival. Indeed there is a further irony in the fact that Saul's fate is precisely what he has sought for David

Notes to Chapter Five

("What is my sin before your father that he seeks my life?").

15   While the reader may feel at first sight that the sentiment does not match well with, for example, 19:1 (Saul asks Jonathan to kill David) and 19:9ff. (Saul tries himself to kill David with his spear), on reflection it is seen to fit with the last scene involving Jonathan and Saul, namely 19:6f. (when Saul assures Jonathan that David shall not be put to death).

16   Noted also by Jobling (1978:25, n.16) who himself makes so many perceptive observations on this material.

17   Note a pattern in the text that warns us of the probable future of Jonathan's initiative. In 18:1-3, his love for, and covenant with, David is followed rapidly by Saul's destructive anger (verse 8). Here the same pattern occurs in 20:17 and verse 30.

18   On the deception of Ahimelech, both the impiety involved and the responsibility of David for the resulting bloodshed (chapter 22), see McKane's comments and ethical evaluation (pp.134ff.). As far as the "impiety" is concerned it needs to be stressed, in the context of a comparison with Saul, that the sense of the passage is that David does break the religious rules, as his lie about "going on an expedition" makes evident. (And so Jesus - though taking David's part - understood the text, according to Matt 12:3f., Mark 2:25f., Luke 6:3f.). However, unlike Saul's "impiety" at Gilgal, David's at Nob brings no rebuff from Yahweh. Rather it is the innocent Ahimelech and the priests of Nob who pay the price of his action.

19   I am speaking in "literary" terms, of course, Whether historically it was a different occasion is not my concern; some scholars would see here what is sometimes called a "doublet" (two versions of the same event).

20   Cf.: (a.1) Doeg's information, which in the context of Saul's anger and accusations of conspiracy, makes it seem absolutely clear that Ahimelech had aided and abetted the fleeing David; (a.2) the apparent breaking of the hrm-commandment, 15:19. Thus when Samuel meets Saul, just as when Saul meets Ahimelech, the decision is, in a sense, already made.

21   Note the way tension is created by God's answer to David's question.

David says: (a)   Will the men of Keilah surrender me?
                       (b)   Will Saul come down?
God answers: (b)   He will come down.
So David has to ask again,
                       (a)   Will the men of Keilah...etc?
before God answers:
                       (a)   They <u>will</u>.
It is the question (a) that <u>is,</u> of course, crucial to David.

22   Note again the symmetry in the prose: with only a couple of exceptions the focus swings rapidly from Saul to David and back again (and so on), each sentence on the one character being balanced nicely by a sentence on the other. The balance is only broken by intervention of the crucial messenger's speech which tells Saul to "make haste" [which is what David has been forced to do (verse 26)] and "come; for the Philistines have made a raid on the land".

NOTES TO CHAPTER SIX

1   Some critics (and cf., for example, the NEB) have chosen to rearrange the text here because, it is claimed, the narrative "does not follow the natural order" (Smith, 217). The point is that, apparently, David's reply should precede rather than follow his action. This is a case of the critic imposing a somewhat pedestrian logic on a nice piece of dramatic prose. I owe some of my conviction on the quality of the MT here to Robert P. Gordon's recent paper on the subject (to a meeting of the [British] Society for Old Testament Study, July 1979) which also discussed some of the overtones and verbal plays in this segment of text. (See also note 23, below.)

2   Cf., for example, Hos 4:1-3, Isa 3:13-5, 41:4; 41:21-4; 43:9-13. For constructive understanding of this tension in the depiction of God, see Nielsen, 74-83.

3   The words are Jonathan's; David assents to them (verse 17). On this point and the textual problems, see Hertzberg, 169 and 173f.; Driver, 164-6.

4   As far as Michal is concerned, however, it remains only "promise": as a daughter of the house of Saul she will have her marriage to David cut short (24:44) and the "cutting off" theme carries over into 2 Samuel when she is returned to David but depicted as continuing childless to the day of her death (2 Sam 6:23). Jonathan's exclusive devotion to David is certainly the case in our story. Elsewhere, however, he is said to have produced a child (2 Sam 4:4, 9:3; cf. 1 Chron 8:34, 9:40).

5   Cf. Deut 27:20 ("Cursed by he who lies with his father's wife, because he has uncovered his father's kānāp"; cf. 22:30 [MT, 23:1]) where kānāp is often treated as a metaphor for "wife", taking the two clauses in the verse as "synonymous parallelism" (on which, see above, n.8 to

153

Chapter Five). But because of the verb "uncover", the term
is much better taken as a euphemism for the genitals, either
those of the wife, or, perhaps more likely (given the nature
of a kānāp as an "extremity"), those of the father. If the
latter, the clause is a rather succint way of making the
point that, in having intercourse with his father's wife, a son
is (unlawfully) taking his father's place; he is, as it were,
uncovering his father's penis when he uncovers his own
before the wife, for the law can contemplate no other penis
in these circumstances than that of the husband/father.
    The other place where kānāp is very likely to have a
sexual overtone is in Ruth 3. Ruth is told to uncover Boaz's
"feet/legs" (a singular translation of the word is also
possible: the form, from rgl, is an unusual one) and to lie
down/sleep by him; when he awakes she asks him to "spread
[his] kānāp over her". What subsequently happens is then
conveniently masked by the all-purpose verb, škb ("lie down,
lie with, sleep with", etc.). The passage is delightfully
ambiguous. But it is undoubtedly redolent with the possibility of sexual interpretation. As Campbell notes (p.121):
"the storyteller meant to be ambiguous and hence provoc-
ative". A euphemistic meaning (as "penis") for kānāp fits
this context extremely well.

6   The RSV translates 24:14 as follows: "After whom has
the king of Israel come out? After whom do you pursue?
After a dead dog! After a flea!". The exclamation marks
suggest that the the outburst is one of genuine humility.
Might it not be equally well punctuated with question
marks? That is to say, are these phrases the sign of genuine
humility, false humility, or rhetorical questions assuming
the answer, "No!"? In this last case there is a hint of threat;
as if to say "You have taken on more than you imagine!".

7   Seven times (good) and seven times (evil); cf. chapter
24: four and three times, respectively; chapter 16: two and
four times respectively.
    It is thus not altogether surprising to find Levenson
describe the chapter as a "moral allegory". His essay is a
particularly stimulating and enjoyable one. As will become
clear, I share some of his main emphases; for example,
Abigail's skilful rhetoric, her concern for her future and her
recognition (the contrast is with Nabal) of David's kingship.

Notes to Chapter Six

The interpretation of the episode as a "moral allegory", however, does present certain problems: in particular it seems to me to ride over the key moral difficulties, namely David's "protection-racket" (as Levenson himself denotes it, p.19); the problem of violence (pp.23f.; and note the analogy Levenson draws with the David of 2 Sam 11); and the death of Nabal (if David is not justified in slaying him, why is God?).

8   I take this phrase to mean a "reckless" person, one who disregards the proprieties or conventions, or disturbs the status quo (cf. Hannah, 1 Sam 1:16; Sheba ben Bichri, 2 Sam 20:1). Cf. Gunn, 1978:104 and n.20.

9   As Levenson notes (p.14), it is hard to imagine that one would name his child "foolish". The implication, therefore, is either that the name is an artificial one, a label for purposes of characterization (or as Levenson nicely puts it "character assassination") or that it is in fact a genuine name, with no meaning other than its "nameness". In this latter case it would perhaps have once had a somewhat different form and would almost certainly have meant, when it meant anything, something other than "foolish". (Names which come to equate morphologically with what seem to be inappropriate words are not an uncommon feature of languages; and just because when this happens it provides an unfailing source of humour, often barbed, people with such names do, on occasion, change them.) It seems to me (against Levenson) that this latter alternative is more likely, given that no other character has an obviously contrived name and that such "overt characterization" suggests a degree of unsubtlety which is not characteristic of this narrative. Rather the narrator uses the play on the possible meaning of the name as one way of manipulating the reader's evaluation of the character (and through him, the others), without allowing the reader the privilege of having a fixed point of reference (as would be the case if "Nabal" were not in fact a name but only a descriptive label).

What the name meant originally, if my argument is right, I cannot say (cf. Levenson, 14); but neither do we know the original meanings of a good many other names which are undoubtedly names.

10   Any more precise overtones remain quite obscure, I

would maintain. However scholarly endeavour on the subject of nāgîd is considerable and hypotheses about special meanings and development are not few. For a recent survey and re-investigation, see Mettinger, 151-84 ("The Divine Designation and the Problem of Nagid").

11 Note the contrast between the way Abigail receives David's messengers and the way Nabal had received the first group. Nabal, to request for food: David is a mere servant, I am master; Abigail, to request for person: I am the servant of a servant - i.e. David is far more than me.

12 Note the nice ambiguity in Abigail's last line (the term "my master") - it can be taken not only as referring to David, but also as suggesting something like "When Nabal has received his just deserts from Yahweh!".

13 While seeing in Nabal the pattern of Saul's experience we might observe also that in some respects Abigail's behaviour is reminiscent of Jonathan's behaviour earlier: note her secret meeting with David, her designation of him as her "master" and "prince" (cf. Jonathan's designation of David as "king") and her interest in her future place with David (cf. Jonathan, "And I shall be next to you").

The parallel between Nabal and Saul is also observed (p.37) in Miscall's recent article (which came to my attention too late for me to take detailed account of it), which briefly explores 1 Sam 25 in relation both to its context in 1 Samuel and to some other biblical stories (Gen 12, 20, 26 and 2 Sam 11f.). This is a stimulating essay which takes seriously the "moral" dimension of the material, and in doing so raises various questions vis-à-vis my own interpretation.

14 Note the touch of irony in the use of "As Yahweh lives, you deserve to die"; and cf. earlier in the scene, verse 10, and 13:39.

15 We may remember that Saul had seen the "stirring up" rather differently (22:7f.).

16 For a different interpretation of Saul's fainting, see Beuken, 11-3.

17 Note the "ring-composition" (the first sentence of an episode or scene is repeated at the end, thus creating a

"loop"). This gets us back to the main story line (the Philistine attack). Cf. 28:1,4 + the story of Endor + 29:1.

18   Gronbaek (pp.51, 60f., 202) also observes the connection of chapters 15 and 30 through the "booty" motif (and cf. Mettinger, 34), but his interest is rather different from mine: he uses his observation to draw traditio-historical conclusions about the modification and development of various component traditions in the text prior to their incorporation in the present text.

19   In another sense, Saul could be said to have been killed by Yahweh "by the hand of the Philistines" - as Saul had hoped to do to David.

20   Saul's kingship begins on a "high place": and ends on mount Gilboa with the news being carried to the "house of their idols" (reading MT) and his armour (symbolic of his status as king and champion of Israel) to the temple of Ashtaroth. His death is thus a desecration. It is a cruel fate for one who had struggled to worship loyally the one god, Yahweh.

21   As the text stands, the Amalekite is lying when he claims responsibility for Sauls's death. (On the question of whether there are traces here of originally separate sources, see, for example, Gronbaek, 216-21; Gunn, 1978:130 n.51). There is a certain bitter irony in the involvement of the Amalekite here. Saul really cannot win against these most hated of Israel's foes. He defeats them in battle but they provide the occasion for his undoing, nevertheless (chapter 15); he bravely takes his own life, but as far as the living (and that includes his rival, David) are concerned, he ends with his life in hock to one of these hated people - is reduced to begging an Amalekite to kill him. Had that been true it would have been a sufficient irony; for it to be untrue but thought to be true is to add an extra twist to the picture of a Saul who could not win.

22   David's lament deserves an extended analysis in its own right. For present purposes, however, I am content to observe that it can be both moving and ironical. To take just one or two examples. The repeated reference to the slaying of Israel's "glory" (Saul and Jonathan) upon the "high places" conjures up the picture of a sacrifice, which is, indeed, one

interpretation of what has happened. Saul (and his son) are a sacrifice to Yahweh - on which see further, Chapter Seven. "The shield of Saul, not anointed with oil": an oblique expression of death, but also a metaphorical indication of Saul's failure as "messiah"! "Saul and Jonathan...In life and in death they were not divided": fine rhetoric, covering a less than happy reality! "They were swifter than eagles": but David was swifter! "How are the mighty fallen": but another "mighty" has arisen!

23With my book "in press" I have received from Robert P. Gordon a copy of a paper on 1 Samuel 24-6 which is highly pertinent to the discussion of these chapters above. I have not had time to consider properly his argument and the extent to which our conclusions in fact match. However it is clear that while his overall perspective is a little different (the focus is upon David, with a quite extensive assessment of his function and character) he makes many similar observations, in some cases offering a more detailed analysis than I have done. One central point we share is expressed in the following sentences: "Narrative analogy is a device whereby the narrator can provide an internal commentary on the action which he is describing, usually by means of cross-reference to an earlier action or speech. Thus narratives are made to interact in ways which may not be immediately apparent; ironic parallelism abounds wherever this technique is applied. Narrative analogy, we submit, provides an important clue to the relationship between 1 Samuel 25, which tells the story of Nabal, and the contiguous chapters, which treat of David's sparing of Saul. The point can be expressed in the simple equation: Nabal=Saul. Saul does not vanish from view in 1 Samuel 25; he is Nabal's alter ego". The paper, entitled "David's Rise and Saul's Demise: Narrative Analogy in 1 Samuel 24-26", is to be published later this year (1980) in The Tyndale Bulletin.

NOTES TO CHAPTER SEVEN

1   One way of doing this is to "double" various other characters in the play as witches. Lady Macbeth is the most obvious candidate, but various combinations including servants, the porter of Act II and the Act III murderers can be effective.

2   Also in para 4.1 on p.22. There is a rather crucial ambiguity in the sentence I have quoted ("ignorance of this"); some difficulty for me in deciding whether the term "know" (etc.) is being used strictly or in the sense of "accept"; and whether the reference is to Saul's rejection or David's designation.

3   Although the fact remains that in the text the question of "acceptance" is in principle tied up with the question of David in particular.

4   For further explorations on this theme see Brueggemann, 167ff.

5   Note, however, that the text does not allow us to draw conclusions about whether this process of self-vindication through the manipulation of Saul is a matter of conscious decision, the play of deep-seated (unconscious) feelings, or both. It simply observes the crucial shift in attitude towards the monarchy, details Saul's misfortune, and makes clear the connection between the people's rejections of Yahweh and Yahweh's rejection of Saul.

6   There is then (on my interpretation of the whole story) a nice equivalence: the provision of the (earthly) king involves repentance on the parts of both the people and Yahweh.

7   That is to say, the theological problems which these scholars have isolated can be linked and restated in terms which are less anchored to Israel's peculiar history and

institutions and more immediately relevant to the reader who does not share that setting and those particular concerns.

8   We are now obviously touching the edges of issues that must concern any who wish to explore a theistic interpretation of their own existence. I beg the indulgence of the reader who has perhaps, and with justification, expected not just a few throw-away hints but a substantial examination of the way my interpretation of the Saul story (especially the implications for an understanding of the nature of God) might relate not only to other biblical material but to other streams of theology in the "biblical" tradition. To do that, however, would be in effect to start another book and I have chosen to settle for a more modest goal. As a gesture to the reader who wishes to take some further steps in these directions may I observe that the following (to make a drastic selection) have proved pertinent and thought-provoking in a variety of ways in my recent reading: Crenshaw (1969) on questioning the justice of God in ancient Israel; Hayman, on theological reflection on the problem of evil in Rabbinic Judaism; Thompson's useful review (pp.5-82) of Old Testament and intertestamental views on the origin of evil and the responsibility for it; Simundson's thoughtful and readable book (with the layman much in mind) on biblical responses to the question of suffering. And I would note finally that a discussion of a "repenting" God might well find stimulus in contemporary "process" theology (cf. Griffin's book specifically).

BIBLIOGRAPHY

Ackerman, James
    1974 (See Gros Louis)
Ackroyd, Peter R.
    1971 The First Book of Samuel, Cambridge Bible Com-
           mentary on the NEB; Cambridge: C.U.P.
    1975 "The verb love - ' āhēb in the David-Jonathan
           narratives", VT 25: 213f.
Arnold, Matthew
    1895 "The Study of Poetry", Essays in Criticism. Second
           Series, London.
Barr, James
    1973 "The Bible as Literature", in The Bible in the
           Modern World (Chapter Four), New York: Harper &
           Row.
    1976 "Story and History in Biblical Theology", Journal of
           Religion 56: 1-17.
Berg, Sandra Beth
    1979 The Book of Esther, SBLDS 44; Missoula: Scholars
           Press.
Beuken, W.A.M.
    1978 "I Samuel 28: The Prophet as Hammer of Witches",
           JSOT 6: 3-17.
Birch, Bruce B.
    1976 The Rise of the Israelite Monarchy: The Growth
           and Development of 1 Samuel 7-15, SBLDS 27; Mis-
           soula: Scholars Press.
Blaikie, W.G.
    1892 The First Book of Samuel. Expositors Bible; London.
Blenkinsopp, Joseph
    1975 "The Quest of the Historical Saul", in J.W.
           Flanagan, A.W. Robinson, eds., No Famine in the
           Land. Studies in honor of John L. McKenzie, Mis-
           soula: Scholars Press. Pp.75-99.

King Saul: Bibliography

Braulik, G.
1970   "Aufbrechen von geprägten Wortverbindungen und Zusammenfassen von stereotypen Ausdrücken in der alttestamentliche Kunstprosa", Semitics 1: 7-11.
Brueggemann, Walter
1977   The Land. Place as Gift, Promise, and Challenge in Biblical Faith, Outlines to Biblical Theology; Philadelphia: Fortress.
Buss, Martin
1979   "Understanding Communiction", in M. Buss, ed., Encounter with the Text. Form and History in the Hebrew Bible, Semeia Supplements; Philadelphia: Fortress, Missoula: Scholars Press. Pp.3-44.
Campbell, Edward F.
1975   Ruth, Anchor Bible; Garden City, New York: Doubleday.
Chappell, Clovis G.
1925   Sermons on Old Testament Characters, New York: Harper.
Clines, David J.A.
1978   The Theme of the Pentateuch, JSOT Supplement Series 10; Sheffield: JSOT Press.
Coggins, R.J.
1979   "History and Story in Old Testament Study", JSOT 11: 36-46.
Conroy, Charles
1978   Absalom Absalom! Narrative and Language in 2 Sam. 13-20, Analecta Biblica 81; Rome: Biblical Institute Press.
Crenshaw, James L.
1969   "Popular Questioning of the Justice of God in Ancient Israel", ZAW 82: 380-95. [Reprinted in Crenshaw, ed., Studies in Ancient Israelite Wisdom, Ktav; 1976: 289-304].
1978   Samson. A secret betrayed, a vow ignored, Atlanta: John Knox.
Dietrich, W.
1972   Prophetie und Geschichte. Eine redaktionsgeschichtliche Untersuchung zum deuteronomistischen Geschichtswerk, FRLANT 108; Göttingen: Vandenhoek und Ruprecht.

Bibliography

Driver, S.R.
1913   Notes on the Hebrew Text and the Topography of the Books of Samuel, 2nd edn.; Oxford.

Fishbane, Michael
1979   Text and Structure. Close Readings of Selected Biblical Texts, New York: Schocken Books.

Gagarin, Michael
1976   Aeschylaean Drama, Berkeley: University of California Press.

Ginzberg, Louis
1913   The Legends of the Jews, Vol.IV; Philadelphia: Jewish Publication Society of America. [Reprint 1968].

Goldman, S.
1951   Samuel, Soncino Books of the Bible; London: Soncino Press.

Good, Edwin M.
1965   Irony in the Old Testament, Philadelphia: Westminster Press.

Gosselin, E.A.
1976   The King's Progress to Jerusalem. Some Interpretations of David during the Reformation Period and Their Patristic and Medieval Background, Humanita Civilitas 2; Malibu, California: Undena Publications.

Gottwald, Norman K.
1959   "Saul", in A Light to the Nations, New York: Harper. Pp. 184-91.
1976   "War, Holy", in IDB Supplement Volume, Nashville: Abingdon. Pp. 942-4.

Griffin, David Ray
1976   God, Power, and Evil: A Process Theodicy, Philadelphia: Westminster.

Grønbaek, Jakob H.
1971   Die Geschichte vom Aufstieg Davids (1 Sam. 15-2 Sam. 5): Tradition und Komposition, Copenhagen: Munksgaard.

Gros Louis, Kenneth R.R., James S. Ackerman, Thayer S. Warshaw, eds.,
1974   Literary Interpretations of Biblical Narratives, Nashville: Abingdon.

Gunn, David M.
1978   The Story of King David: Genre and Interpretation, JSOT Supplement Series 6; Sheffield: JSOT Press.
Hastings, James
1914   "Saul", "Jonathan", "David", in The Greater Men and Women of the Bible, Vol.III; London. Pp. 63-160.
Hayes, John H.
1979   An Introduction to Old Testament Study, Nashville: Abingdon.
Hayman, A.P.
1976   "Rabbinic Judaism and the Problem of Evil", Scottish Journal of Theology 29: 461-76.
Hertzberg, Hans Wilhelm
1964   I & II Samuel. A Commentary, trans. by J.S.Bowden (from the 2nd German edn., 1960); The Old Testament Library; London: SCM.
Humphreys, W. Lee
1978   "The Tragedy of King Saul: A Study of the Structure of 1 Samuel 9-31", JSOT 6: 18-27.
Jobling, David
1976   "Saul's Fall and Jonathan's Rise: Tradition and Redaction in 1 Samuel 14:1-46", JBL 95: 367-76.
1978   "Jonathan: A Structural Study in 1 Samuel", in The Sense of Biblical Narrative, JSOT Supplement Series 7; Sheffield: JSOT Press.
Jones, Gw.H.
1975   "'Holy War' or 'Yahweh War'?", VT 25: 642-58.
Kennedy, A.R.S.
1904   Samuel, Century Bible; Edinburgh.
Kessler, Martin
1970   "Narrative Technique in 1 Samuel 16", CBQ 32: 543-54.
1974   "A Methodological Setting for Rhetorical Criticism", Semitics 4: 22-36.
Kitto, H.D.F.
1956   Form and Meaning in Drama. A Study of Six Greek Plays and of Hamlet, London: Methuen.
Knierim, Rolf
1968   "The Messianic Concept in the First Book of Samuel", in F. Thomas Trotter, ed., Jesus and the Historian, Philadelphia: Westminster Press.

Bibliography

Koch, Klaus
1969   The Growth of the Biblical Tradition. The Form-
        Critical Method, trans. by S.M.Cupitt (from 2nd
        German edn. 1967); London: A. & C. Black.
König, E.
1900   Stylistik, Rhetorik, Poetik in Bezug auf die Bib-
        lische Litteratur, Leipzig.
Lemche, Niels Peter
1978   "David's Rise", JSOT 10: 2-25.
Levenson, Jon D.
1978   "1 Samuel 25 as Literature and as History", CBQ
        40: 11-28.
Mauchline, John
1971   1 and 2 Samuel, New Century Bible; London: Oli-
        phants.
Mayes, A.D.H.
1978   "The Rise of the Israelite Monarchy", ZAW 90: 1-19.
McCarthy, Dennis J.
1973   "The Inauguration of the Monarchy in Israel. A
        Form-Critical Study of 1 Samuel 8-12", Inter-
        pretation 27: 401-12.
McKane, William
1963   I & II Samuel, Torch Bible; London: SCM
McKenzie, John L.
1962   "The Four Samuels", Biblical Research 7: 3-18.
Melamed, Ezra Zion
1961   "Break-up of Stereotype Phrases as an Artistic
        Device in Biblical Poetry", in C. Rabin, ed., Studies
        in the Bible, Scripta Hierosolymitana 3; Jerusalem:
        Magnes Press. Pp. 115-53.
Mettinger, Tryggve N.D.
1976   King and Messiah. The Civil and Sacral Legitima-
        tion of the Israelite Kings, Coniectanea Biblica;
        Lund: Gleerup.
Miscall, Peter D.
1979   "Literary Unity in Old Testament Narrative", in
        R.C. Culley, ed., Perspectives on Old Testament
        Narrative, Semeia 15; Missoula: Scholars Press.
        Pp. 27-44.
Myers, J.M.
1962   "Saul, son of Kish", in IDB, Vol.IV, 228-33.

King Saul: Bibliography

Newman, John Henry
1868 "Sermon III. Saul", and "Sermon III. The Trial of
Saul", in Plain and Parochial Sermons, Vol.III,
16-28, and Vol.VIII, 33-47, respectively; new edn.;
London.
Nielsen, Kirsten
1978 Yahweh as Prosecutor and Judge, JSOT Supplement
Series 9; Sheffield: JSOT Press.
Polzin, Robert
1979 "Literary Unity in Old Testament Narrative: A
Response", in Culley, ed., Perspectives in Old
Testament Narrative (see Miscall). Pp. 45-50.
von Rad, Gerhard
1951 Der Heilige Krieg im alten Israel, Zürich.
1962 Old Testament Theology, Vol.I; trans. by D.M.G.
Stalker (from 2nd German edn.); Edinburgh: Oliver
and Boyd.
Ridout, Samuel
1972 King Saul, The Man After the Flesh, Sunbury,
Penn.: Believers Bookshelf. [Originally pub. by
Loizeaux Bros., Neptune N.J., no date (c. 1900)].
Robertson, David
1977 The Old Testament and the Literary Critic, Guides
to Biblical Scholarship; Philadelphia: Fortress.
Robinson, Thomas
1790 "The Character of Saul", in Scripture Characters or
a Practical Improvement of the Principal Histories
from the Time of the Judges to the End of the Old
Testament, London. Pp. 33-66.
Simundson, Daniel
1980 Faith Under Fire, Minneapolis: Augsburg Publishing
House.
Smith, Henry Preserved
1899 A Critical and Exegetical Commentary on the
Books of Samuel, International Critical Commentary; Edinburgh.
Soggin, J. Alberto
1967 Das Königtum in Israel, Beihefte ZAW; Berlin: de
Gruyter.
1976 Introduction to the Old Testament, trans. John
Bowden (from 2nd Italian edn. 1974); London: SCM.

Bibliography

Stoebe, Hans Joachim
  1973 Das erste Buch Samuelis, Kommentar zum alten
        Testament VIII i; Gütersloh: Gerd Mohn.
Thompson, Alden T.
  1977 Responsibility for Evil in the Theodicy of IV Ezra,
        SBLDS 29; Missoula: Scholars Press.
Thompson, J.A.
  1974 "The Significance of the verb love in the
        David-Jonathan Narratives in 1 Samuel", VT 24:
        334-8
Warshaw, Thayer S.
  1974 (see Gros Louis)
Weippert, M.
  1972 "'Heiliger Krieg' in Israel und Assyrien", ZAW 84:
        460-93.
Weiser, Artur
  1936 "1 Samuel 15", ZAW 54: 1-28.
Welch, Adam C.
  1952 "Saul", in Kings and Prophets of Israel, London:
        Lutterworth. Pp. 63-79.
White, Hugh C.
  1979 "Structural Analysis of the Old Testament Narr-
        atives", in Buss, ed., Encounter with the Text (see
        Buss). Pp. 45-66.
Whitelam, Keith W.
  1979 The Just King. Monarchical Judicial Authority in
        Ancient Israel, JSOT Supplement Series 12; Shef-
        field: JSOT Press.
Wilberforce, Samuel
  1870 Heroes of Hebrew History, London.
Willis, John T.
  1973 "The Function of Comprehensive Anticipatory Re-
        dactional Joints in I Samuel 16-18", ZAW 85:
        294-314.
Wilson, Robert R.
  1979 "Prophecy and Ecstasy: A Reexamination", JBL 98:
        321-37.

ABBREVIATIONS

CBQ	Catholic Biblical Quarterly
IDB	The Interpreter's Dictionary of the Bible
JBL	Journal of Biblical Literature
JSOT	Journal for the Study of the Old Testament
LXX	The Septuagint (ancient Greek version of the Old Testament)
MT	The Massoretic Text (ancient Hebrew text of the Old Testament)
NEB	The New English Bible
RSV	The Revised Standard Version (of the Bible, in English)
SBLDS	Society of Biblical Literature, Dissertation Series
VT	Vetus Testamentum
ZAW	Zeitschrift für die alttestamentliche Wissenschaft

INDEX OF AUTHORS

INDEX OF PASSAGES IN SAMUEL

Index of Passages in Samuel

Index of Passages in Samuel

King Saul: Indexes

INDEX OF SUBJECTS